ACCOUNTING FOR SMALL MANUFACTURERS

Small Business Management Series
Rick Stephan Hayes, Editor

Simplified Accounting for Non-Accountants
  by Rick Stephan Hayes and C. Richard Baker

How to Finance Your Small Business with Government Money: SBA Loans
  by Rick Stephan Hayes and John Cotton Howell

Accounting for Small Manufacturers
  by C. Richard Baker and Rick Stephan Hayes

Simplified Accounting for Engineering and Technical Consultants
  by Rick Stephan Hayes and C. Richard Baker

ACCOUNTING FOR SMALL MANUFACTURERS

C. RICHARD BAKER

RICK STEPHAN HAYES

A Ronald Press Publication

JOHN WILEY & SONS
New York • Chichester • Brisbane • Toronto

Library of Congress Cataloging in Publication Data

Baker, C Richard, 1946-
    Accounting for small manufacturers.

    (Wiley series on small business management)
    "A Ronald Press publication."
    Includes index.
    1. Accounting.   2. Small business.   I. Hayes, Rich
Stephan, 1946-   joint author.   II. Title.   III.
Series.
HF5635.B1613   657'.9042   80-12001
ISBN 0-471-05704-5

Printed in the United States of America

10 9 8 7 6 5 4 3 2 1

Preface

There are thousands of small manufacturing enterprises in the United States today, which make products ranging from food to spaceship components. Despite the proliferation of big business, it is still possible for an entrepreneur to conceive of a product, design and manufacture it, and make a lot of money. This book should help the entrepreneur-manager to keep some of that money and to maintain the business on a sound financial footing while waiting for the first million to roll in.

The purpose of the book is to aid the owner-manager and chief financial officer of the small manufacturing enterprise to better manage his or her business from a financial perspective. The essential tool of financial management is a set of well organized and properly kept accounting records. This book shows you:

- How to organize your business for accounting and income tax purposes.
- What the output of the accounting information system will be (i.e. financial statements).
- How to design and keep accounting records.

The book also:

- Defines and discusses the major assets and liabilities of the small manufacturing enterprise.
- Provides tips for managing assets more effectively and reducing liabilities to manageable levels.

Even if your goal is not to be extremely rich, but simply to run your business better, a knowledge of accounting principles and practices will help. The SBA has published a series of management aids for the small manufacturer with this in mind.

One particularly useful management aid is called "Business Plan for Small Manufacturers." A business plan helps the owner-manager of a business enterprise to assess his or her position and to develop an overall strategy with respect to the business. The business plan is an essential starting point. We reproduce the SBA business plan, which is a management aid, in its entirety in Appendix 1. We encourage you to go through it carefully, filling in the blanks. If this is done conscientiously, it will help you better understand your company and its environment. It will set the stage for a fuller appreciation of the material covered in this book.

Appendix 2 reproduces a pamphlet published by the American Institute of Certified Public Accountants. It discusses the advantages and disadvantages of going public.

C. Richard Baker
Rick Stephan Hayes

New York, New York
Topanga, California
March 1980

Contents

ACCOUNTING FOR SMALL MANUFACTURERS

Chapter One

Forms of Doing Business for the Small Manufacturing Enterprise

The principal forms of business organizations for a small manufacturing operation are: (1) The sole proprietorship, (2) the partnership, and (3) the corporation. There are also hybrid forms such as joint ventures, Sub-Chapter-S corporations, and limited partnerships.

SOLE PROPRIETORSHIP

A sole proprietorship is the most basic form of business organization. You and your business are indistinguishable for legal accounting and tax purposes. Your personal assets and your business assets are in effect co-mingled, and your business income and nonbusiness income are reported to the Internal Revenue Service on the same tax form, Form 1040. Business income is simply segregated on Schedule C of Form 1040. About the only thing you need to start business as a sole proprietor is a license to do business in the area in which you choose to operate.

Assuming that your sole proprietorship is a bona fide business at which you are attempting to make a living, there are certain tax advantages of this business form.

First, legitimate business expenses are tax deductible. This includes depreciation on property used in the business; necessary operating expenses such as heat, light, power, telephone; reasonable travel and entertainment; and so on. Salaries and wages paid to employees of your business are tax deductible expenses. Furthermore, other legitimate deductions may be available.

Very few small manufacturers would actually want to operate their businesses as sole proprietorships for very long, because of various legal and tax problems and because of the necessity to raise capital.

Advantages of the Sole Proprietorship*

• *Ease of formation.*   There are less formality and fewer legal restrictions associated with establishing a sole proprietorship. It needs little or no governmental approval and is usually less expensive than a partnership or corporation.

*Adapted from "Selecting the Legal Structure for Your Firm," *MA 231*, Management Aids for Small Manufacturers, U. S. Small Business Administration.

- *Sole ownership of profits.*   The proprietor is not required to share profits with anyone.
- *Control and decision making vested in one owner.*   There are no co-owners or partners to consult.
- *Flexibility.*   Management is able to quickly respond to business needs in the form of day to day management decisions as governed by various laws and good sense.
- *Relative freedom from government control and special taxation.*

Disadvantages of the Sole Proprietorship*

- *Unlimited liability.*   The individual proprietor is responsible for the full amount of business debts which may exceed the proprietor's total investment. This liability extends to all the proprietor's assets, such as house and car. Additional problems of liability, such as physical loss or personal injury may be lessened by obtaining proper insurance coverage.
- *Unstable business life.*   The enterprise may be crippled or terminated upon illness or death of the owner.
- *Less available capital, ordinarily, than in other types of business organizations.*
- *Relative difficulty in obtaining long-term financing.*
- *Relatively limited viewpoint and experience.*   This is more often the case with one owner than with several.

PARTNERSHIP

A partnership can be nothing more than two or more sole proprietors who have agreed to pool their assets and operate a business jointly. There does not have to be a formal agreement between the partners in order for a partnership to exist legally, or for tax purposes. However, most states have partnership laws. Written partnership agreements ordinarily should be drawn up by a lawyer in conformity with the laws of your particular state. For federal income tax purposes, a partnership includes not only a partnership as it is known in common law, but also a syndicate, group, pool, joint venture, or other unincorporated organization that carries on any business and that is not defined as a trust, an estate, or a corporation.

A partnership is not taxable as such. The individual members of the partnership pay taxes on their shares of the partnership taxable income, whether this income is distributed to them or not.

Example.   A partnership is composed of two partners sharing profits equally. In the current year, the taxable income of the business is $30,000, none of which is distributed to the partners. The partnership tax return will report the $30,000 and show shares of $15,000 to each of the partners. Each partner will report his share of the partnership taxable income on his own tax return, even though the income has not been distributed to him.

The character of the income earned by a partnership is not altered when the income passes to the partners. For example, if a partnership sells a building and realizes a long-term capital gain on the transaction, the long-term capital gain is passed through to the partners rather than being reflected as part of the partnership income. The

*Adapted from "Selecting the Legal Structure for Your Firm," *MA 231*, Management Aids for Small Manufacturers. U. S. Small Business Administration.

types of income, losses, and expenses which are passed to partners include ordinary income and loss, dividends, interest, short-term capital gains, long-term capital gains, and charitable contributions.

Limited Partnership

A limited partnership is a special type of partnership authorized under many state laws. A limited partnership must have at least one general partner, who has unlimited liability for the debts of the partnership, and who is responsible for managing the business. The limited partners are only liable to the extent of their partnership interests; they must not participate in any way in the management of the business. The advantage of a limited partnership is that it may employ leverage on the limited partners' invested capital to earn a higher rate of return than would ordinarily be possible.

Example.   A contractor becomes the general partner in a limited partnership. He agrees to acquire land, construct a building, and sell the building when it is completed. He arranges for five investors to contribute $20,000 each to the project in exchange for limited partnership interests. On the basis of the construction plans and the $100,000 equity, the contractor-general partner is able to arrange a bank loan for $200,000. The loan will be secured by a purchase money mortgage and a performance bond. Most of the money contributed by the limited partners, and even that which was borrowed, is treated as a tax deductible expense in the year of the formation of the partnership. This type of arrangement is often called a tax shelter.

Congress has felt that the proliferation of tax shelters is not appropriate, and in the Tax Reform Act of 1976, tax shelters were curtailed. Basically, the rule against tax shelters became such that the amount of losses that would be claimed from certain investment activities could not exceed the total amount that the taxpayer had "at risk" in the partnership. Under the "at risk" rule, loss deductions are limited to the amount of cash contributed to the partnership by the partner. Since there is no liability for the limited partners beyond their initial investment, that is all they can deduct on their tax returns.

There is a place for limited partnerships in small manufacturing operations, particularly in the case where one partner wants to actually run the operation and the other partner just wants to be a passive investor. Also, in the start-up phase a small manufacturing operation may be structured as a limited partnership so that operating losses may be passed through to the individual investors.

Advantages of the Partnership*

- *Ease of formation.*   Legal formalities and expenses are few compared with the requirements for creation of a corporation.
- *Direct rewards.*   Partners are motivated to apply their best abilities by direct sharing of the profits.
- *Growth and performance facilitated.* In a partnership, it is often possible to obtain more capital and a better range of skills than in a sole proprietorship.
- *Flexibility.*   A partnership may be relatively more flexible in the decision making process than in a corporation. But, it may be less so than in a sole proprietorship.
- *Relative freedom from government control and special taxation.*

*Adapted from "Selecting the Legal Structure for Your Firm," *MA 231*, Management Aids for Small Manufacturers, U.S. Small Business Administration.

Disadvantages of a Partnership*

- *Unlimited liability of at least one partner.* Insurance considerations such as those mentioned in the proprietorship section apply here also.
- *Unstable life.* Elimination of any partner constitutes automatic dissolution of partnership. However, operation of the business can continue based on the right of survivorship and possible creation of a new partnership. Partnership insurance might be considered.
- *Relative difficulty in obtaining large sums of capital.* This is particularly true of long term financing when compared to a corporation. However, opportunities are probably greater than in a proprietorship by using individual partners' assets.
- *Firm bound by the acts of just one partner as agent.*
- *Difficulty of disposing of partnership.* The buying out of a partner may be difficult unless specifically arranged for in the written agreement.

SUB-CHAPTER S CORPORATIONS

In the eyes of the law, a corporation is a person, and it can sue, be sued, and must pay taxes. Since the individuals who own the corporation also pay taxes on any dividends they receive from the corporation, there is double taxation.

Many people argue that this double taxation should be eliminated. To a certain extent it has been eliminated by the creation of small business corporations, also referred to as tax option corporations or Sub-Chapter S corporations.

A Sub-Chapter S corporation is a corporation that has elected, by unanimous consent of its shareholders, not to pay any corporate tax on its income. Instead, the shareholders pay taxes on this income, even though it is not distributed. Shareholders of a Sub-Chapter S corporation are entitled to deduct, on their individual returns, their share of any net operating loss sustained by the corporations.

Unlike a partnership, a Sub-Chapter S corporation is not a conduit. That is, individual items of income and deduction are not passed through to the shareholders to retain the same characteristics in the hands of those shareholders as they had in the hands of the corporation. Instead, taxable income is computed at the corporate level just as it is computed for any other corporation. The shareholders are then taxed directly on this taxable income, whether or not the corporation makes any distributions to them. There is one exception to this no conduit rule: the Sub-Chapter S corporation's net capital gains or losses on their individual returns.

Only a domestic corporation that is not a member of an affiliated group can elect Sub-Chapter S status. A qualifying Sub-Chapter S corporation may have no more than one class or stock and no more than 15 shareholders. The shareholders must all be individuals, or estates of deceased individuals who were shareholders when they died.

The tax aspects of a Sub-Chapter S corporation are somewhat complex. If you decide that Sub-Chapter S status is an appropriate form of business organization for your small manufacturing business, you should consult a certified public accountant or an attorney.

*Adapted from "Selecting the Legal Structure for Your Firm," MA 231, Management Aids for Small Manufacturers, U. S. Small Business Administration.

CORPORATIONS

Most businesses that are not designed strictly for investment purposes eventually decide to incorporate. The reasons for this include: limited personal liability of owner-managers, financing and growth flexibility, and transferability of interest.

The first decision faced by persons who would like to incorporate a business is *where* to incorporate. Some state corporation laws are more attractive to incorporators than others. For example, there are many business incorporated in Delaware, but not all of them actually do business there. This is because Delaware has had, for many years, a corporation law that offers incorporators certain privileges, advantages, and facilities for incorporation that could not be obtained elsewhere.

Recently, however, differences in corporation laws among the major commercial states have been reduced and it is often preferable to incorporate in the state where the majority of the business will be done.

Although the procedure of incorporation varies in detail from state to state, the pattern is much the same everywhere. Certain steps should be taken before the incorporators draw up a charter. These steps include discovering a business opportunity, investigating that opportunity, developing financial and promotional arrangements, arranging for property and material supply, solicitation of preincorporation stock subscriptions, and reservation of a corporate name (See Figure 1.1).

Corporate Charters

Corporate charters are required to have certain clauses, and permitted to have others (See Figure 1.2). Usually the first clause of a corporate charter is the corporate name. The name cannot conflict with any other name used in that state. Names of individual incorporators should not be used because those individuals risk losing the right to use their own names for business purposes.

A second clause will contain the business purpose: the objects or general nature of the business. Many states permit a purpose clause to state that the corporation is formed for any lawful purpose.

A third clause of the corporate charter will outline the capital structure of the proposed corporation, including the authorized number of shares, the rights, preferences, privileges, and restrictions on the various classes and series of shares, whether the shares have a par value, and the voting rights of the shares.

Other clauses in the charter pertain to the location of the principal office, the number of directors, the names and addresses of the original directors, the duration

	Sole Proprietorship	Partnership	Sub-Chapter S Corporation	Corporation
Net profit of company taxed as owner's individual income	yes	yes	yes	no
Owners have legal liability	yes	yes	no	no
Company tax deductions (conduit transaction)	yes	yes	no	no
Corporate division of an affiliated group			no	yes
Has more than one class of voting stock			no	yes
More than 15 stockholders			no	yes
Stock can be held by other corporations			no	yes

Figure 1.1   Comparison of business types.

CHARTER

Corporate name
Business purpose
Capital structure
Location of principal office
Number of shares
Number of directors
Names and addresses of directors
Existence of preemptive rights
Specific and collective rights
Others

BYLAWS

Duties and compensation of corporate officers
Qualification of membership on board of directors
Director committees
Date and place of annual stockholder meeting
Provision for audits
Others

Figure 1.2   Corporate charter.

of the corporation, the existence of preemptive rights, the powers of directors, a statement that the corporation may become a partner in a partnership, and other provisions.

The bylaws of a corporation deal with the internal management rules of the corporation. They must be consistent with the charter of the corporation. Bylaws usually deal with matters such as the duties and compensation of corporation officers, the qualifications for membership on the board of directors, executive and other director committees, the date and place of annual shareholders meetings, provisions for audits, and other matters.

The financing of a corporation is accomplished primarily through two means: debt and equity. Debt financing is discussed in Chapter 6.

Equity financing of a corporation is obtained through issuance of common stock or preferred stock.

The rights of the holders of common stock in a business corporation are established by the laws of the state in which the corporation is chartered and by the terms of the charters. The terms of charters are relatively uniform on many matters, some of which have been described previously.

In addition, the following two matters are usually addressed in corporate charters with respect to rights of common stockholders.

Collective Rights.   Certain collective rights are usually given to the holders of common stock. Some of the more important rights allow stockholders to amend the charter, to adopt bylaws, to elect directors, to authorize sale of major assets, to enter into mergers, to change the amount of authorized common stock, and to issue preferred stock, debentures, bonds, and other securities.

Specific Rights.   Holders of common stock also have specific rights, as do individuals owners. They have the right to inspect the corporate books.

Advantages of the Corporation*

- *Limitation of the stockholder's liability to a fixed amount, usually the amount of investment.* However, do not confuse corporate liability with appropriate liability insurance considerations.
- *Ownership is readily transferable.*
- *Separate legal existence.*
- *Stability and relative permanence of existence.* For example, in the case of illness, death, or other cause for loss of a principal (officer), the corporation continues to exist and do business.
- *Relative ease of securing capital in large amounts from many investors.* Capital may be acquired through the issuance of various stocks and long term bonds. There is relative ease in securing long-term financing from lending institutions by taking advantage of corporate assets and often personal assets of stockholders and principals as guarantors. (Personal guarantees are very often required by lenders).
- *Delegated authority.* Centralized control is secured when owners delegate authority to hired managers, although they are often one and the same.
- *The ability of the corporation to draw on the expertise and skills of more than one individual.*

Disadvantages of the Corporation*

- *Activities limited by the charter and by various laws.* However, some states do allow very broad charters.
- *Manipulation.* Minority stockholders are sometimes exploited.
- *Extensive government regulations and burdensome local, state, and federal reports.*
- *Indirect reward (less incentive) if manager does not share in profits.*
- *Considerable expense in formation of corporation.*
- *Numerous and sometimes excessive taxes.*

Advantages and Disadvantages of Common Stock Financing

There are four principal advantages of using common stock as a source of financing for a corporation:

1. Common stock does not entail fixed charges. As the company generates earnings, it can pay common stock dividends. In contrast to bond interest, there is no legal obligation to pay dividends.
2. Common stock carries no fixed maturity date.
3. Since common stock provides a cushion against losses for creditors, the sale of common stock increases the credit worthiness of the firm.
4. Common stock may at times be sold more easily than debt: common stock may have a higher expected return because in a period of inflation the return will increase whereas the return on debt will remain constant.

*From "Selecting the Legal Structure for Your Firms," *MA 231*, Management Aids for Small Manufacturers, U.S. Small Business Administration.

There are several disadvantages of using common stock as a source of financing for a corporation:

1. The sale of common stock extends voting rights or control to the additional stockholders. For this reason, additional equity financing is often avoided by small and new firms. The owner-managers may be unwilling to share control of their companies with outsiders.

2. Common stock gives more owners the right to share in profits. The use of debt may enable the company to employ funds at a fixed low cost, whereas common stock gives equal rights to new stockholders to share in the net profits of the company.

3. The costs of underwriting and distributing common stock are usually higher than for underwriting and distributing preferred stock or debt. Underwriting costs are higher because the costs of investigating an equity security investment are greater than for a comparable debt security. Also, because common stocks are more risky, equity holdings must be diversified. This means that a given dollar amount of new stock must be sold to a greater number of purchasers than the same amount of debt.

4. Common stock dividends are not deductible for tax purposes, but bond interest is.

Par and No Par Stock

Common stock either has a par value assigned to it by the issuing company, or it is no par stock. Par value is an arbitrary amount assigned to a share of stock and has no necessary relationship to its market value at any given time. For accounting purposes, no par stock is assigned a stated value per share by the issuing company, and this is the basis on which the stock is presented in the balance sheet.

At the time stock is sold initially the price received in excess of either the par or stated value is entered in an account entitled "Paid-in Surplus," "Capital Surplus," or "Capital in Excess of Par or Stated Value," in the balance sheet.

Preferred Stock

Preferred stock has claims or rights ahead of common stock, but behind those of debt securities. The preference may be a prior claim on earnings; it may take the form of a prior claim on assets in the event of liquidation; or it may take a preferential position with regard to both earnings and assets. The hybrid nature of preferred stock becomes apparent when one tries to classify it in relation to debt securities and common stocks. The priority feature, and the fixed dividend, indicate that preferred stock is similar to debt. Payments to preferred stockholders are limited in amount, so that common stockholders receive the advantages or disadvantages of leverage. However, if the preferred dividends are not earned, the company can forego paying the dividends. In this way, preferred stock is similar to common stock.

TRANSFORMING THE STRUCTURE OF A BUSINESS

One of the few remaining ways to become rich in the United States is to start a business enterprise, make it successful, take the company public in a stock offering (retaining a healthy share of the stock yourself), and then see the stock rise significantly in price in the public market (see Appendix 2). This is, of course, a long shot gamble; but if you win . . .

Some lawyers, accountants, and investment bankers make a specialty of taking new companies into the public markets. Their goal is to be part of the long shot when it comes through. The tax implications of moving away from proprietorship and partnership toward a corporation are such that generally accepted accounting principles (such as concepts of accrual, depreciation, inventory, etc.) are more frequently brought into play in corporations. The business manager in a corporate setting has to be more aware of his accounting options, and the business's accountant has to be more aware, not just of taxes, but of generally accepted standards of accounting and auditing.

When a corporation decides to go into a public issue of stock, it may want to do many things from an accounting standpoint. For example, in a private company saving taxes is paramount, whereas in a public company saving taxes is important, but reported earnings may be equally important. Therefore, a company moving from private to public status may want to reassess its depreciation and amortization policy along with other accounting treatments, such as bad debt allowances, warranty reserves, inventory valuation, and so on.

Going public may mean that your company will be audited for the first time by a certified public accountant. Many local accountants are highly competent at tax returns, tax planning, and preparing financial reports from client records, but they may be infrequently engaged to perform certified audits. It is generally not possible for a CPA who is closely allied with your business as an advisor and preparer of financial statements to perform a certified audit. Going public often means you have to find a new CPA firm. This can be costly and somewhat traumatic. The benefit is a general assurance that your financial statements are prepared in conformity with generally accepted accounting principles. Such conformity, plus a unqualified opinion from a respected CPA firm, will enhance the marketability of the stock of your company. This means more money if your stock is sold successfully.

A public issue of stock requires several outside consultants, notably an accountant and a lawyer with prior experience in public securities offerings, and a securities underwriter or investment banker. The accountant must prepare a certified audit opinion upon completion of his or her audit of your business.

Typically, no documents will be required by the SEC if the total funds raised are less than $100,000. If the total funds raised are between $100,000 and $1,500,000, you may be able to avoid filing many of these documents by complying with Regulation A of the Securities Act of 1933, which specifies an exemption for small offerings. If the total funds raised are over $1,500,000, it will probably be necessary to undergo a complete registration statement procedure. The registration statement will be filed with, and reviewed by, the SEC in Washington, D.C., or a regional field office.

Upon completion of the review, the registration is said to "go effective" and your stock may be legally sold in the public markets. This is where the underwriter plays a role in the issuance and sale. His or her job is to judge the movement of the market and to estimate the best time to begin selling the stock in the public market. As a fee the underwriter typically receives a certain percentage of the total amount raised, or alternatively he or she will purchase the new stock at a price which is estimated to be below the market price when the stock is sold publicly. In the latter case, the risk of stock price decline is often on the underwriter, which is the reason for the name "underwriter."

Most companies that are initially required to file registration statements in conjunction with sales of stock will be compelled to file additional annual, quarterly, and other update reports and to revise their registration statements, prospectuses, and proxy materials from time to time. This is an added cost in terms of the time involved for management, accountant's and lawyer's fees, and probable printing costs. Such costs should be considered when initially planning a public issue of stock or other securities.

Chapter Two

Financial Statements for the Small Manufacturing Enterprise

Business financial statements include: (1) the income statement (profit and loss statement), (2) the statement of financial condition (balance sheet), and (3) the statement of retained earnings and the funds flow statement,

The financial statements are the culmination of the accounting process.

The most used of the financial statements is the income statement—the IRS requires an income statement for all businesses. The income statement is a summary of money that came into the business (revenue or income), money that was spent (cost of sales and expenses), and how much money remained after costs were paid (net profit).

The next most widely used financial statement is the balance sheet. The IRS does not require that partnerships and proprietorships file a balance sheet with their income tax returns. Because the IRS does not require them, many small businesses do not understand or use balance sheets. The balance sheet is a summary of what the business owns (assets), what it owes (liabilities), and how much of the owner's money is in the business (owner's equity).

To explain the difference between balance sheet and income statement, the analogy of a moving train is often used.

Let's assume that there are two photographers assigned to photograph a train. One photographer chooses to use a 35mm still camera. The other will use a movie camera.

The train moves through the countryside and the still photographer waits at a bridge crossing. When the train arrives at the bridge, he takes a snapshot of the train. This is a picture of the train at one moment in time.

The movie photographer, on the other hand, travels alongside the train and films it from the time it leaves the station until it arrives at the bridge. This is a picture of the train over a period of time.

The still photo that was taken at the bridge is similar to a balance sheet. It is a picture of the train at one moment in time. The balance sheet is a picture of a business at one moment in time—at the end of a period. It shows how many assets the business has, how much it owes, and how much the owner(s) have put into the business at a certain date.

The moving picture of the train from the station to the bridge is like an income statement. An income statement measures costs and expenses against sales revenue over a period of time. It shows the operation of the business and the profit over an *entire period.*

Since the balance sheet is a statement of one moment in time, it is headed with the date. For example:

Hero Manufacturing Company
Statement of Financial Condition
January 31, 1980

The income statement, on the other hand, is for a continuous period ending on the date of the financial statement. Therefore, the income statement date is prefaced with the words "for the period ending. . . ." For example:

Hero Manufacturing Company
Income Statement
For the Period Ending January 31, 1980

The statement of retained earnings and the funds flow statement are not used as much as the balance sheet and income statement and most small business people know very little about them. The IRS does *not* require a statement of retained earnings or funds flow statement to be included in any business's income tax. If your company has a CPA who is doing an audited statement, generally accepted accounting principles require that he or she include these financial statements.

Retained earnings is the amount of money that is taken from net profit to be put back into the business. Retained earnings are what is left over from net profit after tax, dividends, owner's draw, and other items are taken out. Funds are defined either as amount of working capital (current assets minus current liabilities) or cash.

By stretching the train example you can get the idea of what the statement of retained earnings and the funds flow statement measure in a business. Assume that the train has a certain amount of coal to stoke the engine when it starts. Every so often, as its supply gets low, it stops to pick up more coal. The coal is constantly burned up and has to be replaced. Besides using the coal for running the engine, the engineer may use the coal to heat the train.

At the beginning of the train trip the train had a certain amount of coal, and along the route it picked up some more. During the trip it used coal and at the end of the trip it will have a certain amount of coal left over. The engineer keeps an account book summarizing all the sources and uses of coal.

The statement of retained earnings and the funds flow statement are like the engineer's account book. Instead of coal, a business uses cash, working capital, and long-term captial. The statements are a summary of the sources and uses of cash, working capital, and long-term capital.

FINANCIAL STATEMENTS AND THE FIVE GROUPS OF ACCOUNTS

Throughout this book we will discuss five groups of accounts—assets, liabilities, owner's equity, revenue (income), and expenses. These account groups are used in the financial statements. Assets, liabilities, and owner's equity are the three basic account groups in the *balance sheet.* Revenue and expense are the basic account groups in the *income statement.*

The statement of retained earnings or the funds flow statement is the measurement of the sources of business funds and the uses of those funds. It uses both the balance sheet and the income statement accounts.

THE INCOME STATEMENT

An income statement, commonly called "profit and loss statement," consists of revenue and expense accounts. Gross profit (the difference between revenue and cost of sales, which is one of the expense accounts) and net profit (the difference between gross profit and operating expenses) are income statement amounts that are calculated.

A graphic presentation of an income statement can be seen in Figure 2.1. The accounts used (sales (revenue), cost of sales (expenses), and operating expense) have amounts that come directly from the company's books. By subtracting cost of sales, the result is the gross profit. If you subtract the operating expense from the gross profit the result is net profit. An income statement is usually presented in the following format.

	Sales
	Sales
Less:	Cost of sales
Equals:	Gross profit
Less:	Operating expense
Equals:	Net profit

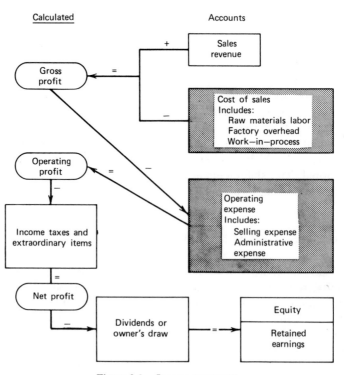

Figure 2.1.   Income statement.

Example.   Hero Manufacturing Company has $100,000 in sales for the year. Hero has $60,000 in costs of sales and $30,000 in operating expense. Hero's income statement would be calculated as follows:

	Sales	$100,000
Less:	Cost of sales	60,000
	Gross profit	$ 40,000
Less:	Operating expense	30,000
	Net profit	$ 10,000

You can also see from Figure 2.1 that some costs, such as taxes, principal loan repayment, and owner's salary or dividends, come out of net profit. Whatever is left after these costs are deducted from net profit becomes *retained earnings*, which is part of the owner's equity on the balance sheet.

Figures 2.2 and 2.3 show income statements from a small manufacturing enterprise. Figure 2.2 shows the basic income statement, while Figure 2.3 shows a supporting schedule of cost of goods manufactured.

HERO MANUFACTURING COMPANY
INCOME STATEMENT
FOR THE YEAR ENDED DECEMBER 31, 1980

Net sales			$669,100
Cost of goods sold			
Finished goods inventory, January 1, 1980		$ 69,200	
Cost of goods manufactured (exhibit 2.3)		569,700	
Total cost of goods available for sale		$638,900	
Less finished goods inventory, Dec. 31, 1980		66,400	
Cost of goods sold			572,500
Gross margin			$ 96,600
Selling and administrative expenses:			
Selling expenses:			
Sales salaries and commissions	$26,700		
Advertising expense	12,900		
Miscellaneous selling expense	2,100		
Total selling expenses		$ 41,700	
Administrative expenses			
Salaries	$27,400		
Miscellaneous administrative expense	4,800		
Total administrative expenses		32,200	
Total selling and administrative expenses			73,900
Net operating profit			$ 22,700
Other revenue			15,300
Net profit before taxes			$ 38,000
Income tax			12,640
Net income after income tax			$ 25,360

Figure 2.2.   Income statement.

HERO MANUFACTURING COMPANY
STATEMENT OF COST OF GOODS MANUFACTURED
FOR THE YEAR ENDED DECEMBER 31, 1980

Work-in-process inventory, January 1, 1980			$ 18,800
Raw materials			
Inventory, January 1, 1980		$154,300	
Purchases		263,520	
Freight In		9,400	
Cost of materials available for use		$427,220	
Less inventory, December 31, 1980		163,120	
Cost of materials used		$264,100	
Direct labor		150,650	
Manufacturing overhead			
Indirect labor	$23,750		
Factory heat, light, and power	89,500		
Factory supplies used	22,100		
Insurance and taxes	8,100		
Depreciation of plant and equipment	35,300		
Total manufacturing overhead		178,750	
Total manufacturing costs			593,500
Total work in process during period			$612,300
Less work-in-process inventory, December 31, 1980			42,600
Cost of goods manufactured			$569,700

Figure 2.3.   Statement of cost of goods manufactured.

Income Statement Accounts

The income statement is made up of three basic sections: sales, cost of sales, and expenses.

Sales includes all sales of products. Sometimes sales are reported as "net sales." Net sales is sales after discounts and allowances (returned sales, payment discounts on accounts receivable).

Cost of sales (cost of goods sold) is the total price paid for the products sold during the accounting period, including freight, labor, and overhead. Retail and wholesale businesses compute cost of goods sold by adding the value of the goods purchased during the period to the beginning inventory, and then subtracting the ending inventory. Manufacturing firms, however, include such items as factory overhead and direct labor in their cost of sales.

Cost of sales includes:

Inventory sold—finished and work-in-process.

Raw materials

Factory overhead

Freight-in

Raw material purchases

Subcontract work

Factory salaries and labor

Operating expense includes general and administrative, selling, and shipping expenses, although sometimes businesses list these groups of expenses separately. General and administrative expense (sometimes simply called G&A) includes utilities, salaries, supplies, rents, and other operating costs necessary to the overall administration of the business. Selling expense includes salaries of the sales force, commissions, advertising expense, and the like. Other activities which contribute to the company sales activities are rent, heat, light, power, supplies, and other items.

Operating expense includes:

Wages and salaries

Rental expense

Repairs and maintenance

Depreciation

Bad debt

Travel and transportation

Business entertainment

Interest

Insurance

Taxes

Licenses

Utilities

Supplies

Advertising

Charitable contributions

Accounting, legal, and consulting

Franchise, trademark, or trade name expenses

Educational expenses for employees of the company

Some businesses receive additional income from interest, dividends, miscellaneous sales, rents, royalties, gains on sales of assets, and so on. In these cases, the "net profit" is really net operating profit and is referred to as such. The "other income" is added to the net operating profit and any "extraordinary costs"—such as loss on sales of assets—will be subtracted from it.

THE BALANCE SHEET

A balance sheet (statement of financial condition) is a summary of what a business owns (assets) and what claims there are against those assets—liabilities (creditors' claims) and equity (the owner's claim.)

The balance sheet is summarized in the form of the basic accounting equation:

$$\text{Assets} = \text{Liabilities} + \text{Equity}$$

The balance sheet is based on historical costs. Assets are stated on the balance sheet (1) the lower of their original cost (less depreciation or amortization) or (2) net realizable value. Common and preferred stock is recorded at the original amount received for the stock. Liabilities are recorded at the amount owed at the end of that accounting period.

The reason for using historical cost is that is reduces to a minimum the extent to which the accounts are affected by the personal opinions of the owners. For example, if the value of assets was set at the present market value, persons responsible for the accounts would have to appraise the current market value. Of course, different

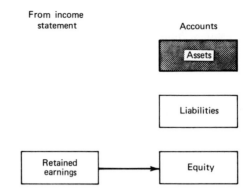

Figure 2.4.   Balance sheet (statement of financial conditions).

people have different ideas as to what market value is. Therefore, if market value were used, two companies with identical forklifts might carry the asset at $8000 in one case and $10,000 in another.

Balance Sheet Examples

Figure 2.4 shows the three account groups that make up the balance sheet: assets, liabilities, and equity. Notice that there is no computation required in a balance sheet as in an income statement. The statement is fully represented by the accounts on the books. Notice from the exhibit that "retained earnings" from the income statement is incorporated into the equity position.

Figure 2.5 is a sample balance sheet. This shows the typical categories and items of a balance sheet. Assets are on the left (or presented first) and liabilities and equity are on the right (or presented last). The first listed assets are the current assets. The first listed liabilities are the current liabilities. Current assets are assets that can be converted to cash within one year. Current liabilities are debts which must be repaid within one year.

Current assets are followed by a group of asset called "fixed assets" and by another group called "other assets." "Fixed assets" are assets which will be useful for more than one year and generally (with the exception of land) are depreciable or amortizable assets. "Other assets" are not included in the balance sheet of every company. They are assets that can not be converted to cash within one year and usually are not depreciable or amortizable. "Other assets" also includes such assets as patents and intangibles which are amortized.

After current liabilities comes "long-term liabilities." Long-term liabilities are debts that will be paid in more than one year.

The equity (or capital) portion of the balance sheet shows the basic components of the owner's investment and retention of capital in the business: stock, paid-in surplus, and retained earnings. In proprietorships and partnerships, this section may only contain the owners' cumulative equity in the business (owners' equity) and the retained earnings for that period (sometimes just stated as "net profit").

Balance Sheet Accounts

An *asset* is property that is used in the trade or business. This property contributes toward earning the income of the business, either directly or indirectly. Assets are productive items which contribute to income and are generally tangible property or

HERO MANUFACTURING COMPANY
BALANCE SHEET
DECEMBER 31, 1980

ASSETS:

Current Assets		
Cash	$ 12,000	
Accounts receivable	119,000	
Notes receivable	7,800	
Inventories	235,200	
Prepaid expenses	26,000	
Total Current Assets		$ 400,000
Fixed Assets		
Land	45,000	
Buildings and improvements	230,000	
Equipment and vehicles	497,000	
Furniture and fixtures	31,456	
Less: Accumulated Deprec.	(212,456)	
Total Fixed Assets		$ 591,000
Other Assets		
Investments	49,000	
Goodwill	76,000	
Research and development	31,000	
Total Other Assets		$ 156,000
Total Assets		$1,147,000

LIABILITIES:

Current Liabilities		
Accounts payable	$ 98,500	
Notes payable	7,340	
Accrued taxes	103,182	
Accrued salaries	66,640	
Total Current Liabilities		$ 275,662
Long-Term Liabilities:		
Notes payable	28,503	
Bonds (8-½% due 1985)	310,635	
Total Long-Term Liabilities		$ 339,138
Total Liabilities		$ 611,800
EQUITY		
Capital stock	100,000	
Paid-in surplus	120,000	
Retained earnings	315,200	
Total Equity		$ 535,200
Total Liabilities and Equity		$1,147,000

Figure 2.5.   Balance sheet.

promises of future receipt of cash (accounts receivable, investments, etc.). Chapters 4 and 5 explain assets in detail. Assets include:

Cash
Accounts and notes receivable
Inventory
Investments
Prepaid expense
Equipment
Automobile
Land and buildings
Leasehold improvements
Furniture and fixtures
Patents
Goodwill
Research and development

Liabilities include all debt of the company. See Chapter 6 for a detailed description. Liabilities include:

Accounts payable
Notes payable
Accrued expenses (taxes, salaries, etc.)
Bonds
Mortgages

Equity (capital) is the amount of money that the owners have invested in the company. This includes the amount they started the company with (initial capital) plus all money that has accumulated in the company since its inception. Capital includes:

Owners' stock or initial contribution
Paid-in surplus (for corporations)
Retained earnings

STATEMENT OF RETAINED EARNINGS AND FUNDS FLOW STATEMENT

The statement of retained earnings is concerned with determining retained earnings at the end of a period. The funds flow statement includes the results of the statement of retained earnings, but it goes further by explaining movements of cash during the period.

Neither the statement of retained earnings nor the funds flow statement is required for income tax purposes, but both are required according to "generally accepted accounting principles" set down by the Financial Accounting Standards Board, which is the body primarily responsible for promulgating generally accepted accounting principles. Publicly held companies are generally required to have these statements as part of their financial reporting procedures.

Statement of Retained Earnings

Most corporation are required to show their retained earnings in a "Statement of Retained Earnings" (See Figure 2.6). This financial statement shows the retained earnings at the beginning of the period (the end of the *last* period), adjustments made during the accounting period, and the retained earnings at the end of the present period.

Adjustments made during the period include:

1. Profit or loss from the period after taxes.
2. Dividends or owners' draw.
3. Adjustments resulting from transactions in the company's own capital stock (buying treasury stock).
4. Transfers to and from accounts properly designated as appropriated retained earnings, such as contingency reserves.

The Funds Flow Statement

Publicly held companies are required to have a funds flow statemtent along with their income statement and balance sheet. The funds flow statement traces the flow of working capital during the accounting period. Working capital is the excess of current assets over current liabilities.

The funds flow statement answers some of the following questions.

1. Where did profits go?
2. Why were dividends not larger in view of the profits made?
3. How was it possible to distribute dividends when the company has net operating loss?
4. How was the expansion in plant and equipment financed?
5. What happened to the sale of additional stock and the proceeds from the sale of fixed assets?
6. How was the retirement of debt accomplished?
7. What brought about the increase or decrease in working capital?

HERO MANUFACTURING COMPANY
STATEMENT OF RETAINED EARNINGS
FOR THE PERIOD ENDED
DECEMBER 31, 1980

Retained earnings, January 1, 1980		$299,840
Add:	Net income	46,210
Less:	Dividends declared	(30,850)
Retained earnings, December 31, 1980		$315,200

Figure 2.6   Statement of retained earnings.

Sources of Funds	Application of Funds
Increase in liabilities	*Decrease* in liabilities
Loans	Pay off loans
Mortgages	Pay off mortgages
Increases in owner's equity	*Decrease* in owner's equity
Owner cash injection	Withdrawals by owners
Stock sales	Dividends
Increase in retained earnings	Net loss
Decreases in fixed assets	*Increase* in fixed assets
Sales of fixed assets	Purchase equipment,
Depreciation	furniture and fix-
	tures, land and
	buildings

Figure 2.7   Funds flow statement.

Figure 2.7 shows how the funds flow statement can be divided into sources of funds and application of funds. Notice that working capital is a *source* of funds when there is (1) an *increase* in liabilities or owner's equity, or (2) a *decrease* in fixed assets. Funds are used (*applied*) when there is (1) a *decrease* in liabilities or owner's equity, or (2) an *increase* in fixed assets.

Examples of sources of funds are: loans and mortgages, injection of ownership cash into the business (stock or owners' capital injection), or increase in retained earnings from the previous year (from Statement of Retained Earnings). Funds sources also include: a decrease in fixed assets, such as sales of equipment or other fixed assets.

Funds are used (applied): to pay off loans and mortgages (decrease liabilities), for withdrawals by owners through dividends or owners' draw, or by decreases in retained earnings resulting from net losses or other cash expenditures. Funds are also used to increase fixed assets, such as equipment, buildings, etc. An example of a funds statement is shown in Figure 2.8.

HERO MANUFACTURING COMPANY
FUNDS STATEMENT
FOR THE PERIOD ENDING
DECEMBER 31, 1980

SOURCE OF FUNDS

Operations: Net income	$25,360	
Add back noncash expenses		
(depreciation)	5,676	$31,036
Sale of stock		10,000
Total sources		$41,036

USE OF FUNDS

Purchase of fixed assets	$ 4,750	
Cash dividends paid	10,000	
Retiremtnt of long-term debt	17,812	$32,562
Net increase in working capital		$ 8,474

Figure 2.8   Funds statement.

SUMMARY

This chapter has introduced the reader to the basic financial statements for a small manufacturing enterprise. The financial statements are the income statement, balance sheet, statement of retained earnings, and funds flow statement.

Financial statements are the output of the accounting information system. The following chapters will show how the accounting information system works to produce financial statements.

Chapter Three
Bookkeeping—Part I

Business "books" and records have evolved over the last 5000 years, primarily through systemization. The first act of systemization was to record transactions of the business in one book on a sequential basis (that is, as the transaction occurred). This book was called the *journal*.

Recording in this book was called journalizing or making journal entries. The bookkeeper had another book that kept track of original transactions under the headings of the type of transaction (sales, expense, asset, etc.). For example, this book kept all the expenses for rent under the heading "rent." This type of book was called a *ledger*.

Business persons quickly found that the original documents (sales slips, invoices, etc.) of business transactions were not enough to ensure accuracy. They needed records that were in one place so they could review at a glance all the transactions for the previous period. These records were the journal and the ledger.

THE FIVE MAJOR GROUPS OF ACCOUNTS

When the bookkeeper began putting certain similar entries under headings in a ledger, he must have used headings like rent, equipment, inventory, sales, and so on, with no consideration of how these accounts might be categorized into similar "groups" of accounts.

Accounting quickly becomes quite complex, with perhaps hundreds of separate account headings. In order to simplify accounting and make it more useful, bookkeepers began looking for group headings. If several account headings—such as rent, supplies, salaries, utilities, advertising, and so on—can be put under a group heading such as *expenses*, life is made simpler. It is also easier for the person who isn't an accountant to understand how the business has done financially.

From this need for simplification, accountants have combined all accounts under group headings. This allows them to set aside whole sections of ledgers for specific types of accounts.

All accounts used by a business can be grouped under the five major headings: assets, liabilities, equity, revenue, and expenses. We have defined these major groups of accounts in Chapter 2.

After grouping of accounts the next development in business recordkeeping was the invention of a way to keep all the accounts in balance. This was accomplished through the use of a balancing mechanism called debits and credits, or double-entry bookkeeping.

Bookkeeping in the Middle Ages was complex and probably confusing. Bookkeepers make mistakes, and if three entries have to be made of the same item (original transaction, journal, and ledger), there are three chances to make mistakes. The question became: "What can be done to minimize these mistakes; to check on each entry so that accuracy is assured?" The system had to be a simple process, one that requires a minimum amount of time, and one that an outside person can easily check.

The idea was simple and elegant. Take one transaction, for example a sale of merchandise, write the number in a positive account and then write the same number in a negative—opposite—account.

There is another factor occurring at the same time. This is that movement in one account causes movement in another account. For instance, if a sale for cash is made, the asset cash increases by an amount equal to sales. It became apparent that all the accounts affected each other, directly or indirectly.

The first double-entry bookkeeping system was the account system of the Genoese communal stewards for the year 1390 AD.

The first book on accounting was printed in Venice in 1494. It bore the title *Summa de Arithmetica, Geometria Proportioni e Proportionalita*, and was written by a Franciscan friar called Fra Luca Pacioli.

In his book Pacioli shows how three books are used in accounting: the memorandum, the journal, and the ledger. His debit and credit usage corresponds with today's usage to a remarkable degree, and he does not fail to advocate a properly classified ledger or to give rules for the correction or erroneous entries. The suggestions for auditing the records, closing them, and carrying them forward are sound today.

Left and Right—The Debit and the Credit

We mentioned briefly the double-entry bookkeeping system. In this system each ledger account has two possible entries, an entry on the left side of the ledger page (debit) and an entry on the right side (credit). Whether a debit entry increases the amount or decreases the amount in an account depends on what account the entry is made in, as we shall discuss shortly. But an entry in the *left* column is always a *debit* and an entry on the *right* side is always a *credit*.

The word debit is from the Latin *debitum* (debt). The word credit is from the Latin verb *credere* (to trust). Most of the early double entry systems were for moneylenders, who had a great need for accuracy and control. If people owe you money you need to know to the penny how much it is. The person who owes you money is likely to forget how much he owes unless you remind him. The moneylender had notes receivable (notes from outside that were due to the money lender). When someone borrowed money, the account with his or her name on it was increased or debited. It was debited because this was the amount *owed (debitum)*. As he or she paid off the account, the account was credited, thus reinforcing the *trust (credit)* of the money lender.

Debit and credit have additional meanings when applied to the different accounts. Some accounts receive a debit entry when they are increased, whereas other accounts are credited to increase them.

This can be summarized as follows:

Account Group	Debit	Credit
Assets	Increase	Decrease
Expense	Increase	Decrease
Revenue	Decrease	Increase
Liabilities	Decrease	Increase
Equity	Decrease	Increase

In accounting if you debit one account you must credit another account. Conversely, if you credit one account you must debit another account. In this way, transactions or movements in one account cause movements in another account. When an owner puts some cash into the business, the accountant wants to keep track of two facts: (1) how much the owner put in, and (2) how much there is in the cash account because of this transaction. If the transaction were written in a journal, it would look like this:

Date	Explanation	Debit	Credit
1/20/80	Cash	$5000	
	Owner's equity		$5000
	To record the contribution		
	of cash to the business of		
	Hero Manufacturing		

When a *sale* is made for *cash*, revenue is increased (credit) and cash is increased (debit). The journal entry would look like this:

Date	Explanation	Debit	Credit
1/21/80	Cash	$ 500	
	Sales		$ 500

When an expense is paid, *cash* is decreased (credit) because the expense has to be paid out of cash, and *expense* is increased (debit). The journal entry would look like this:

Date	Explanation	Debit	Credit
1/22/80	Expense	$ 400	
	Cash		$ 400
	To record payment from		
	cash of an expense		

Assume that Hero Manufacturing is able to get inventory on credit; that is, they pay no money for a certain period of time, but they take possession of the inventory. This would create an "account payable." This transaction would increase (credit) accounts payable, which is a liability, and increase (debit) *inventory* which is an asset. The journal entry would look as follows:

Date	Explanation	Debit	Credit
1/23/80	Inventory	$1000	
	Accounts payable		$1000
	To record purchase of		
	inventory on credit.		

These examples give you an idea of the common transactions that occur in accounting.

Generalizations of Account Transactions

From the above discussion of transactions, the following are some helpful generalizations:

1. Every debit requires at least one credit and every credit requires at least one debit.
2. There are three types of transactions between three account groups: increase-decrease, increase-increase, and decrease-decrease.

    a. Cash decreases (credit) whenever a check is written by the business.

    Most checks are written for expense items: debit (increase) expense and credit (decrease) cash.

    The second largest number of checks written is either to purchase inventory for cash (debit inventory, credit cash) or for the payment on accounts payable for merchandise already purchased on credit (debit accounts payable, credit cash).

    Almost every check written for debt repayment has an interest and a principal portion. The interest portion is an expense and the principal portion is considered a reduction in debt (debit interest expense, debit liability, and credit cash).

    Checks are occasionally written for owners' draw or dividends (debit owners draw or debit dividends, credit cash).

    b. With the exception of a reduction in acounts receivable (asset) caused by a payment by a customer, cash is usually increased (debit) by increases in the liabilities or equity. (For example: debit cash, credit liabilities, or debit cash, credit equity). Only rarely is cash increased from a cash rebate on expense or cost of sales or the proceeds from the sale of assets.

The Basic Accounting Equation and Permanent and Temporary Accounts

The basic accounting equation, the formula from which all accounting logic proceeds, is:

$$\text{Assets} = \text{Liabilities} + \text{Equity (owner's capital)}$$

Using the rules of algebra, this can also be stated as:

$$\text{Assets} - \text{Liabilities} = \text{Equity, or}$$
$$\text{Assets} - \text{Equity} = \text{Liabilities, or}$$
$$\text{Assets} - \text{Equity} - \text{Liabilities} = 0 \text{ (zero)}$$

In other words, the total dollar amount of assets equals the total dollar amount of equity plus liabilities. The dollar amount of assets minus the dollar amount of liabilities (or equity) equals the total dollar amount of equity (or liabilities).

Both sides of the equation are in *balance*, the total of one side (assets) equals the total of the other side (liabilities + equity). When these three accounts are put in document form, as a matter of fact, it is called a "balance sheet."

The equation means that the value of the properties a business owns (assets) are equal to the value of the rights in those properties (liabilities and equity). Liabilities are the creditors' (banks, trade, etc.) rights in the business. Equity is the owners' rights in the business. So rights in properties equal properties.

ORIGINAL TRANSACTION DOCUMENTS

The first step for the bookkeeper of today is the same as it was for the bookkeeper of 5000 years ago. He must record and understand the original transaction documents. Original transaction documents include sales slips, cash register receipts, checks, shipping documents, invoices, petty cash slips, deposit slips, and so on, and represent the first recording of a business transaction at the point of exchange.

We will consider these original transaction documents in the order of their common use. The documents can be grouped as follows:

- Sales documents (cash register receipts, sales slips, daily cash summary, and invoices)
- Bank documents (check, check register, deposit slips)
- Petty cash
- Purchasing documents
- Travel and entertainment records
- Payroll records

Sales Documents

Most retail firms use a cash register for handling transactions where cash sales are involved.

Another method of recording sales, usually reserved for larger sale items, is the "*sales slip.*" An illustration of the sales slip appears in Figure 3.1. The first line usually contains the department and/or salesperson number and an indication of whether it is a cash sale or a credit sale. Credit sales are almost always recorded on a sales slip. The sales slip has a place for the name and address of the customer, followed by a space for any delivery instructions (in instances where the company selling the merchandise also ships it). Further spaces are allowed for a description of the item, including quantity, name, unit price, total price, and sometimes inventory number.

The salesperson gives the customer one copy of the sales slip and retains one for the business (more copies are retained if shipping or special orders are required).

The documents for a charge account would include an application record, and a sales invoice or sales slip.

The first step to opening a credit line with a customer (except when a commercial credit card is used) is to obtain certain application information. The application requires information such as address and name, past credit information, income (either company or personal), expected monthly orders, and so on.

The following is an example of a credit application for a business customer:

BUSINESS: Zlapps Tulip Works   TYPE: Tulip Fabricator
             34 Flower Street   MERCHANDISE MOST FREQUENTLY
             Weed, Calif. 90000   ORDERED: f-719 Tulip Stems
SALESMAN: Charles Smit   PURCHASING MAN: Fred Zlapps
LAST YEAR SALES: $3,000,000   LAST YEAR PROFIT: $48,000
D&B RATING: 3A-2   CREDIT LIMIT: $100,000

Bank Documents

The most commonly used bank documents are the *check* and the *deposit slip* (see Figures 3.2 and 3.3). The checks and deposit slips are usually coded at the bottom

HERO MANUFACTURING COMPANY
10 WEST 36th STREET
NEW YORK, N.Y.   10016   **2301**

CUSTOMER'S ORDER NO.		DEPT.		DATE 2 Feb 1980			
NAME	*Jack Smat Corp.*						
ADDRESS	*216 Tom ave, Everywhere*						

SOLD BY *J.Y.*		CASH	C.O.D.	CHARGE	ON ACCT.	MDSE. RETD.	PAID OUT

BAKER-HAYES: BAKER-HAYES: BAKER-HAYES: BAKER-HAYES: BAKER-

10	1	#3642 Dispensers	50/ea	500	00
	2				
	3				
	4				
	5				
	6				
	7				
	8				
	9				
	10				
	11				
	12				
	13				
	14				
	15				
	16				
	17				
	18		500	00	

REC'D BY

**KEEP THIS SLIP
FOR REFERENCE**

Figure 3.1

with the account number of the business so that it can be read by automated equipment. The name and address of the business which has the account are usually printed in the top left-hand corner. The check has a space for the date, the payee (person to whom the check is made out), a signature, and usually a comment space. The deposit slip lists all the currency, coin, and/or checks to be deposited. When checks are listed, they are listed separately with a code located on the top part of the fraction in the upper right-hand corner of a check. The amounts are totaled.

Whenever a check is written by a company, it is usually recorded on a "check stub" or "*check register.*" In the check register (Figure 3.4) the amount of each check, date, check number, payee, and account number or explanation are recorded each time a

HERO MANUFACTURING COMPANY
NEW YORK, NEW YORK 10016

1198

Jan 14 19 81 16-4 / 1220

PAY TO THE ORDER OF *Snobb Supply* $ 518 03/00

Five hundred eighteen and 03/00 DOLLARS

CHEMICAL BANK

FOR *inventory* *John Jones*

⑈001⑈98⑈ ⑆1220⑈0004⑈094⑈0

FOR DEPOSIT ONLY TO
ACCT. #71-37218
Tom Snobb

Figure 3.2

check is written. The check register may also have a space for entering deposits. Deposits are recorded by date, who from, reason, and total.

Note. When depositing checks there are two types of endorsements. One endorsement is simply the signature of the payee (the person to whom the check is made out). The other type of endorsement is the "restrictive endorsement," which indicates the check is for deposit only before the signature.

Other bank documents include *savings account deposit slips* and *withdrawal slips*. Savings account slips require the name of the depositor, account number, date, and total deposited or withdrawn.

A common internal control procedure of a small business is the reconciliation of the bank account. Figure 3.5 shows a simple bank reconciliation.

Petty Cash

Most businesses set aside a small sum of cash for the payment of minor business expenses. This sum of cash is called the "petty cash fund." Items that are usually paid out of petty cash include postage, transportation, telegrams, incidental office supplies, and sometimes parking, duplicating, and entertainment expenses.

When money is paid out of petty cash the receipt is retained by the keeper of the fund and a notation is made indicating the date, the receipt number (if any), to whom it was paid, what expense category it falls under, the account number, and the amount.

The usual procedure is to issue a check for "petty cash" for some dollar amount—say $100—and keep it in an envelope, a cash box, or a cash register. The money is spent for the various cash expenses and recorded accordingly. When fund

HERO MANUFACTURING COMPANY

16-4

DATE __JAN. 15__ 19 __81__

CHECKING ACCOUNT DEPOSIT TICKET

$ 1,318.04

CHEMICAL BANK

CHECKS	DOLLARS	CENTS
1 16-20	412	01
2 4-18	310	73
3 6-71	242	12
4		

35		
36		
Checks	964	86
Currency	321	00
Coin	32	18
TOTAL	1,318	04

Figure 3.3

amount is spent, another check is written for that amount. The amount of the check is entered in the general journal and the amount of each expense is posted to the proper account (postage, parking, entertainment, etc.) in the ledger.

If we wanted to replenish cash amounting to $55.80, we would make the following entry in the journal:

Date	Explanation	Debit	Credit
1/22/80	Postage expense (510)	$11.00	
	Duplicating expense (511)	27.50	
	Parking expense (512)	2.50	
	Entertainment expense (520)	14.80	
	Cash		$55.80
	To record replenishment of petty cash fund and post expenses to proper accounts		

DESCRIPTION OF DEPOSITS

DATE OF DEP.	SOURCE OF ITEM	NATURE OF ITEM	AMOUNT OF ITEM	TOTAL AMOUNT OF DEPOSIT
1/15/81	ED SINALL (ACCT #173)	PMT. ON ACCT.	412 01	
	JOHN BIG (ACCT 195)	✓	310 73	
	S. W. FOX (ACCT 100)	✓	242 12	
	CASH SALES		353 18	
				1,318 04

CHECK NO.	DATE	CHECK ISSUED TO	IN PAYMENT OF	AMOUNT OF CHECK		DATE OF DEPOSIT	AMOUNT OF DEPOSIT	BALANCE
	1981				BALANCE BROUGHT FORWARD →			1,016 72
1198	1/14	SNOBB SUPPLY	invent. (512)	518 03				498 69
1199	✓	ATOMIC EDISON	util. (640)	112 18				386 51
1200	✓	WORLD TELEPHONE	util. (640)	150 12				236 39
	1/15	DEPOSIT REGISTER				1/15	1,318 04	1,554 43

Figure 3.4

Purchasing Documents

Sometimes a business can simply order stock by telephone, but many suppliers require that a firm request merchandise by written order. The form for requesting goods is called a "purchase order." The purchase order is a form sent by the purchaser to another company ordering goods from that company. Purchase orders are usually in triplicate, each sheet of a different color. One copy is sent to the vendor (supplier), the second copy is usually retained for the purchasing company files, and the third is furnished to the receiving department where the goods are to be delivered.

The purchase order usually contains the following information:

- Number of the purchase order
- Name and address of the vendor
- Name and address of where the goods are to be shipped
- Special shipping instructions
- Date
- Quantity, description, and price of the items ordered.

Cash balance per bank statement		$5000
Add: Deposits in transit		200
		$5200
Subtract: Outstanding checks		
	101	$50
	103	25
	104	90
	107	10	175
Cash balance per accounting records		$5025

Figure 3.5 Bank account reconciliation.

When the vendor ships the goods to the buyer, the vendor prepares an invoice, or bill, that he sends to the buyer (see Figure 3.6).

When these invoices are packed with the shipment they are referred to as "packing slips." This invoice transfers rights to property—providing the property is paid for—to the buyer.

Travel and Entertainment Records

Figure 3.7 is an illustration of an expense report for travel and entertainment. It breaks down the cost for 11 separate items, one of which is not tax deductible as an expense. The following items are recorded:

1. *Transportation* includes airfare, trainfare, busfare, or transportation by automobile compensated at some rate per mile. Note that part of the way down the page this item is broken into destination and departure points. If the amount of this transportation cost is over $25.00 receipts should be included, but it is wisest to include receipts no matter what the cost.
2. *Taxi-limousine-carfare* represents the cost of transportation by private or public transport at the destination and departure points. This is also broken down by departure and destination.
3. *Hotel* includes the cost of room at a hotel. Receipts are always required.
4. *Meals–personal* are not deductible.
5. *Telephone-telegraph* are business related communication costs. Whenever possible receipts should be kept for this, too.

Parks Parts Mfg. 2000 Gold Ave. Houston, Tx. 08960					Number 0950		
					Date 2/18/80		
Sold to	Hero Manufacturing Company						
	20 W. 36th Street				Sale *Ed S.*		
	New York, N.Y.				Terms 30 da.		
Shipped to	*Ron Smith*				Customer number		
Address	*Same*		Via *UPS*	—			
2 cases	#3 parts			$50	ea	100	00
3 cases	#1 parts			55	ea	165	00
						265	00

Figure 3.6. Invoice.

EXPENSE REPORT FOR RECORDING I.R.S. DATA

NAME	TERR. OR DEPT.	DATE OF REPORT
JOHN T. SNOBB	SALES MANAGER	1/30/80

PURPOSE OF TRIP: SALE / EMERSON ACCOUNT

DATE OF TRIP — FROM 1/23/80 TO 1/27/80

ITEM	EXPENSE	SUN.	MON. 1/23/80	TUES. 1/24/80	WED. 1/25/80	THUR. 1/26/80	FRI. 1/27/80	SAT.	ITEM TOTALS
* 1	TRANSPORTATION ($25. OR OVER ATT. RECEIPT)		250 00				250 00		500 00
* 2	TAXI - LIMOUSINE - CARFARE		20 00	32 00	6 30	5 00	7 20		70 50
3	HOTEL (ATTACH RECEIPT)		60 00	60 00	60 00	60 00	60 00		300 00
4	MEALS (PERSONAL USE ONLY NO. 11 FOR OTHER)		7 23		3 38	4 15	3 84		18 60
5	TELEPHONE - TELEGRAM			4 12	2 00				6 12
6	LAUNDRY - VALET SERVICE								
* 7	OTHER AUTO PARKING-TOLLS SERVICE - REPAIRS								
8	TIPS - CHECKING - OTHER		4 00	6 00	4 50	7 00	4 00		25 50
9	POSTAGE		3 50	1 83					5 33
* 10	MISCELLANEOUS & GIFTS								
* 11	ENTERTAINMENT			56 38	10 65				67 03
	DAILY TOTALS ⟶		344 73	160 33	86 83	76 15	325 04		993 08

NON-REIMBURSED EXPENDITURES (PERSONAL RECORD) | ACCOUNTING | AMT. ADVANCE

		REMARKS:	
SUN.			
MON.	7 23		$ 1,000.00
TUES.			EXP. ABOVE
WED.	3 38		
THU.	4 15		$ 993.08
FRI.	3 84	CHECKED BY:	DIFFERENCE
SAT.		APPROVED BY:	
TOTAL	18 60	DATE:	$ ⟨6.92⟩

EXPLAIN BELOW IN DETAIL

ITEM		SUN.	MON.	TUE.	WED.	THUR.	FRI.	SAT.
1	FROM		J.F.K.				GEO, FLA.	
	TO		GEO, FLA.				J.F.K.	
	TO							
	TO							
	AUTO MILEAGE							
2	FROM		AIRPORT	HOTEL	HOTEL	HOTEL	HOTEL	
	TO		HOTEL	DOWNTOWN	CITY HALL	INDUST. PARK	AIRPORT	
	FROM		HOTEL	DOWNTOWN	CITY HALL	INDUST. PARK		
	TO		DOWNTOWN	INDUST. PARK	HOTEL	HOTEL		
	FROM		DOWNTOWN	INDUST. PARK				
	TO		HOTEL	HOTEL				

ITEM	DATE	AUTOPARKING, TOLLS, SERVICE, REPAIRS	AMOUNT	ITEM	DATE	ENTERTAINMENT-SHOW CUSTOMER NAME, & TITLE, AMT., PLACE & BUSINESS PUR- POSE $25. OR OVER ATT. RECPT.	AMOUNT
7				11	1/24	T. BIGGS, GEN'L MGR, EMERSON MFG, TONY'S PIZZA, DISCUSS PURCHASE NEW EQUIP	16 13
10		MISC.-SHOW NAME, COST, PURPOSE $25. OR OVER ATT. RECEIPT			1/24	J. EMERSON, PRES. EMERSON MFG, RITZ, NEGOTIATE PURCH.	40 25
					1/25	T. BIGGS, J. EMERSON, DRINKS CORNER GRILL, FINALIZE SALE	10 65

SIGNED X *John T. Snobb*

APPROVED BY X ____ DATE / /

Figure 3.7

32

6. *Laundry-valet* is for laundry cost required by business necessities.

7. *Other auto* includes the cost of tools, parking, service, repairs, and so on. Receipts should be kept. These are itemized in a section at the bottom of the report.

8. *Tips* may be kept track of here.

9. *Postage* for business correspondence is an expense.

10. *Miscellaneous and gifts* should be carefully itemized as to name of recipient, cost, and purpose. Gifts should not be for more than $25 per person per year.

11. *Entertainment expense* requires careful attention to reporting details. In addition to the breakdown at the bottom of the report, the authors suggest that you attach receipts and give particulars as to customer's name and title, place of business, amount, and what was discussed. We would suggest that the reporter go as far as maintaining at least one paragraph summaries of what was discussed at the meeting. If there is further tax restrictions on expense, entertainment expense is the area in which it will most likely occur. But as long as entertainment expense was conducted for business purposes and this is carefully documented, the business person has little to wory about.

Payroll Records

If you have any employees in your business, you have certain obligations to the federal government for payment of payroll taxes and withholding of income taxes. You will probably have similar obligations for payroll and/or withholding taxes to the state and perhaps to the local jurisdictions.

Federal regulations do not prescribe the form in which your payroll records must be kept, but the records should include the following information and documents:

1. The amounts and dates of all wage payments subject to withholding taxes and the amounts withheld.

2. The names, addresses, and occupations of employees receiving payments.

3. The periods of their employment.

4. The periods for which they are paid by you while they are absent because of sickness of personal injuries, and the amount and weekly rate of payments.

5. Their social security account numbers if they are subject to social security tax.

6. Their income-tax withholding exemption certificates.

7. Your employer-identification number.

8. Duplicate copies of returns filed.

9. Dates and amounts of deposits made with government.

Usually, an employee's earnings card is set up for each employee. Every wage payment to the employee is recorded on this card—all the information needed for meeting federal, state, and city requirements relating to payroll and withholding taxes, and all other amounts deducted from the employee's wages.

A number of payroll-records systems are available commercially. Most of these are based on the pegboard or multiple-copy principle. The single writing of a check or payslip to be given to the employee makes a carbon entry on the employee's earnings card and on a payroll summary or journal for each pay period. If you have only one or two employees, it is usually not necessary to have a special payroll system. Paychecks may be entered directly in your cash disbursements journal or on an earnings card for each employee.

There are three types of federal payroll taxes: (1) income taxes withheld, (2) social security taxes, and (3) federal unemployment taxes. IRS *Publication 15*, "Employer's Tax Guide," should be consulted for additional information about employer-employee relationships, what constitutes taxable wages, the treatment of special types of employment and payments, and similar matters.

Income taxes are withheld on all wages paid an employee above a certain minimum. The minimum is governed by the number of exemptions claimed by an employee.

Social security taxes apply to the first $25,900 (in 1980) of wages paid an employee during a year. A percentage deduction (presently 6.13%) from the employee's wages is matched by a *equal amount* in taxes *paid by the employer*.

In addition to taxes withheld from employees' salaries and also paid by the employer, there is a tax that is paid by the employer *only*. This is the federal unemployment tax (FUTA), and is required only of employers who (1) pay wages of $1500 or more in any calendar quarter or (2) employ one or more persons for some portion of at least one day during each of 20 different calendar weeks. The 20 weeks do not have to be consecutive. Individuals on vacation or sick leave are counted as employees in determining the business's status.

The FUTA tax is paid by the employer (no deduction is made from the employee's wages). After 1977, the rate is 3.4% on the first $6000 of wages paid to each employee. If the state unemployment tax rate exceeds 3.4% the FUTA rate is 0.7%.

Using the example from Figure 3.8, a full accounting for the employees taxes and the employer's taxes and payments is shown in the following general journal entry.

Date	Explanation	Debit	Credit
1/7/80	Salary expense — J. Topps	$200.00	
	Social security expense	12.40	
	FUTA (0.7%) expense		
	State unemployment expense	1.40	
	Expense (3.6%)	7.20	
	Cash		$158.50
	Employee deductions		
	Federal withholding payable		21.40
	State disability payable		2.00
	Social security payable		12.40
	State withholding payable		5.70
	Social security payable		12.40
	FUTA payable		1.40
	State unemployment payable		7.20
	To record payable for January 1–7, 1980 and employer's taxes.		

Note that the example of general ledger includes state taxes. In the state of California, for example, the employer or the employee pays three taxes. The employee pays from his salary the state income tax withholding, which differs according to the number of dependants and the employee's salary. This figure is usually determined by a tax table furnished by state government authorities. The employee also pays from his or her salary state disability insurance (1% up to total salary of $11,400 in California). The *employer* must pay state unemployment taxes (3.6% times the salary amount in California). Most other states have similar types of taxes that are paid by the employee, the employer, or both.

EMPLOYER

EMP. NO. 318-92-8550	PAY FOR PERIOD ENDING 1/7/80

EMPLOYEE'S NAME **JO ANNE TOPPS**

DATE HIRED **1/1/80** — DATE DISCHARGED _____

PLACE OF EMPLOYMENT _____   SCHEDULE HOURS THIS PERIOD _____

DAYS AND HOURS WORKED

	SUN.	MON.	TUES.	WED.	THURS.	FRI.	SAT.	TOTAL DAYS	TOTAL HOURS	RATE PER HR.	
HOURS		8	8	8	8	8		5	40	5.00	
OVER TIME											

SALARY (If paid on fixed Weekly or Monthly Basis)

REMUNERATION OTHER THAN CASH (Room, Board, Tips, etc.)

GROSS EARNINGS	200	00

DEDUCTIONS

% WITHHOLDING TAX **TABLE**	21	40
1 % STATE DISABILITY INSURANCE	2	00
6.05 % FED. INS. CONTRIBUTION ACT	12	40
% STATE WITHHOLDING TAX	5	70
TOTAL DEDUCTIONS	41	50
NET EARNINGS	158	50

LESS: REMUNERATION OTHER THAN CASH

☐ BY CASH ☒ BY CHECK NO. 138	NET PAY THIS PERIOD	158	50

I HEREBY CERTIFY THAT THE TIME SHOWN ABOVE IS CORRECT

EMPLOYEE SIGN HERE _**Jo anne Topps**_

4H417 Rediform

Figure 3.8

Notice also in the example that for the employer-paid items (social security, FUTA, and state unemployment), the employer does not pay them in cash every week, but charges them to a payable account that is usually paid quarterly. The employee items (except the net wage amount of $158.50), are also paid quarterly.

If you are required to withhold income tax from wages or are liable for social security taxes in excess of $200 quarterly, you must file a quarterly return, Form 941. Form 941 combines the social security taxes (including hospital insurance) and income tax withholding. Form 941 is used for reporting income tax withheld from wages, tips, annuities, and supplemental unemployment compensation benefits when no FICA coverage is required.

Due dates for the Forms 941 or 941E and the full payment of tax are as follows:

Quarter	Due Dates
January-February-March	April 30
April-May-June	July 31
July-August-Septemker	October 31
October-November-December	January 31, next year

If you are required to make deposits of taxes and you make timely deposits in full payments of the taxes due, you may file your quarterly return on or before the tenth day of the second month following the period for which it is made. In this case the due dates are as follows:

Quarter	Due Dates
January-February-March	May 10
April-May-June	August 10
July-August-September	November 10
October-November-December	February 10 next year

Chapter Four
Bookkeeping—Part II

To make sense of all the thousands of transactions that the average business has during the year, these transactions are entered into a daily book called the *journal*. It allows the business to keep track of all daily transactions in one place. Transactions are recorded sequentially, as they happen.

If a businessperson wants to find out how much they paid for office supplies in the last two months, he or she would still have a problem. Even with the journal, he or she would have to look through every transaction in the last two months to pick out the supplies he or she bought in order to obtain a total. To solve this problem businesses need another book that categorizes everything under specific topics, or accounts. They need a book that has one page called "office supplies" that lists every office supply expense. This summary book has come to be known as a *ledger*.

Figure 4.1 illustrates the transaction sequence from purchase, to original records of the transaction, to "journalizing," to entry in the ledger.

CHART OF ACCOUNTS

A common practice among most businesspersons is to assign various accounts a number in addition to a name. For instance, the cash account could have a number "101" so that when making entries the number could be used instead of writing out the name. Using numbers instead of, or in addition to, names of accounts is not only easier, but it also lends itself very readily to computerization.

The list of account names and numbers is called "a chart of accounts." In developing an index or "chart of accounts," blocks of numbers are assigned to each group of accounts previously discussed. For example, assets are assigned the block of numbers from 100 to 199 (or 1000 to 1999 for large companies with many accounts); liabilities have the numbers 200 to 299 (2000 to 2999); and so.

Chart of Accounts

Account number	Account name
100–199	Assets
101	Cash
110	Accounts receivable
115	Notes receivable

(cont.)

Chart of Accounts

Account number	Account name
120	Prepaid expense
120.1	Prepaid rent
150	Equipment
150.18	1970 Dodge pick-up truck
. . .	Etc.
200–299	Liabilities
201	Accounts payable
201.29	Accounts payable—ABC Co.
211	Notes payable
211.2	Notes payable Bank of Suez
221	Taxes payable
. . .	Etc.
300–399	Owners' Equity
301	Capital stock
310	Preferred stock
330	Retained earnings
. . .	Etc.
400–499	Revenue
401	Income from operations
401.3	Income from Model B Solid State component
401.5	Income from component Accessories
410	Interest income
450	Income from extraordinary items
. . .	Etc.
500–599	Operating Expense
501	Salary expense
501.7	Officer's salary
505	Payroll taxes
505.2	Administrative employees Payroll tax
508	Rent expense
572	Small tool expense
. . .	Etc.
600–699	Cost of Sales Expense
601	Material purchase
601.62	Purchase of steel
610	Factory salaries
610.3	Factory salaries, plant #3
. . .	Etc.

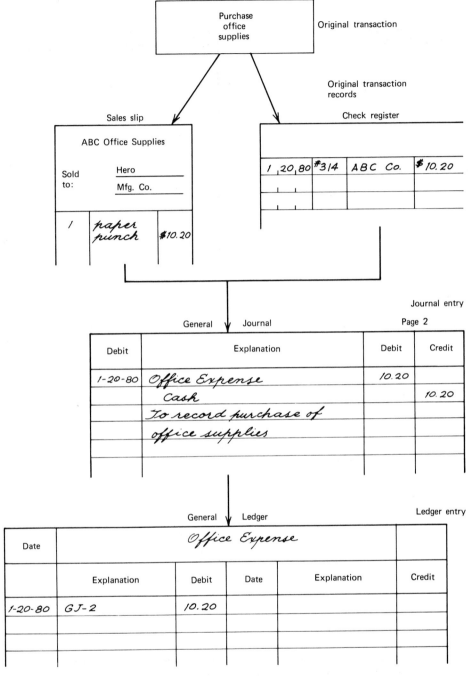

Figure 4.1

JOURNALS (THE DAILY BOOKS)

General Journal

The general journal is the original journal developed to cover all entries. The general journal Figure 4.2 is a form that has a space for the date, a description of the entry, the account number (from the chart of accounts), a check space to check off the entry when it is transferred to the ledger, and spaces for debit or credit entries.

Date	Description	Acct. No.	Debit	Credit

Figure 4.2

Every accounting transaction can be recorded in the general journal. For larger operations with lots of special transactions such as credit sales and purchases and many cash transactions, it is advisable to have the special journals such as the cash disbursements journal, the cash receipts journal, the sales journal and the purchases journal. In these cases where special journals are used, the general journal is only used to record transactions that do not fit into the special journals. For instance, such transactions as recording salaries and taxes or closing out the books at the end of the year would be in the general journal because they have no place in the special journals.

General Journal Examples. John Jones wants to start a circuit manufacturing and distributing company. On January 1, 1980 he deposits everything he has ($25,000) into a business checking account for his new brainchild, Hero Manufacturing. He borrows $25,000 from the Bank Amerigold, and starts setting up his business. Here are some examples of how his general journal will take shape.

Example One. John Jones writes a check from his personal account and deposits it in the checking account of Hero Manufacturing.

The original transaction documents are: a check from his personal account to Hero and a deposit slip. The journal entry would appear as in Figure 4.3.

Date	Description	Acct. No.	Debit	Credit
1980	*1 - 1*			
1/1	Cash	101	25000	
	Owner's Equity	301		25000
	To record cash contribution of John Jones as owner's capital			
	1 - 2			
1/2	Cash	101	25000	
	note Payable - Bank Amerigold	211.1		25000
	To record loan number 378-14 from Bank Amerigold			
	1 - 3			
1/3	Test Equipment	150.1	10000	
	Cash	101		5000
	note Payable - Zarkoff Equip.	211.2		5000
	To record purchase of test equipment from Zarkoff Equipment on credit and for cash			

Figure 4.3

Note that cash is debited (increased) and owner's equity is credited (increased). The transaction involves an increase in an asset (cash) and an increase in equity (owner's equity).

Example Two.   John borrows money from Bank of Amerigold for three years at 11% to start his business.

The original transaction documents are: the loan agreement and a deposit to Hero Manufacturing Company by the bank. The journal entry looks like Figure 4.3.

Cash is debited (increased) by $25,000 and Bank Amerigold note is credited (increased). The transaction involves an increase in an asset (cash) and an increase in a liability (Bank Amerigold note payable).

Example Three.   On January 3 John purchases test equipment from Zarkoff Equipment for $10,000, with a note to Zarkoff for $5000, and a check from Hero Manufacturing for $5000.

The original transaction documents are: a sales slip from Zarkoff Equipment for $10,000, a note to Zarkoff for $5000, and a check from Your Company for $5000. The journal entry is shown in Figure 4.3.

Test equipment is debited (increased) and both cash and notes payable Zarkoff Equipment are credited (cash is decreased and notes payable is increased). The transaction involves both an increase (test equipment) and a decrease (cash) in an asset and an increase in a liability (notes payable—Zarkoff Equipment).

Example Four.   On January 4, Jones buys $30,000 worth of parts inventory from Computer and Circuit Parts Supply Company (CCPSC). He pays cash for $15,000 worth of inventory and takes $15,000 worth of inventory on 30 day credit terms.

The original transaction documents are: a check from Hero Manufacturing for $15,000 and a sales slip from CCPSC for $30,000. The Journal entry is shown in Figure 4.4.

Parts inventory is debited (increased) and cash and accounts payable are credited (decrease cash, increase accounts payable). The transaction involves both an increase (inventory) and decrease (cash) in an asset and an increase in a liability (accounts payable—CCPSC).

Example Five.   Finally, on January 5, Jones has to pay first and last month rent ($1000), a rental commission ($1250), and a security deposit ($1400) for the premises his business will occupy.

The original transaction documents include: the lease, a receipt for the various payments, and a check from Hero. The journal entry is shown in Figure 4.4.

Rent expense, prepaid rent, rental commissions, and deposits are debited (increased), and cash is credited (decreased). The transaction involves both an increase (prepaid rent and deposits) and a decrease (cash) in assets and an increase (rent expense and rental commission) in an expense.

Note.   As illustrated, the standard format of the general journal is to place a heading over each entry with the month (January is 1) and the number of the entry that month (1 through 5 in the example), with the accounts both named and numbered. There is a written summary of the transaction after the separate accounts are shown with the dollar amount of each entry. Also notice that the traditional method is to show the debits first, and the credits last. The debits are flush to the left and the credits are indented.

Date	Description	Acct No.	Debit	Credit
	1-4			
1/4	Inventory - Parts	130	30000	
	Cash	101		15000
	Accounts Payable - CCPSC	201.1		15000
	To record purchase of parts inventory from CCPSC for cash and credit			
	1-5			
1/5	Rent Expense	508	500	
	Pre-Paid Rent	120.1	500	
	Rental Commission	509	1250	
	Deposits	122	1400	
	Cash	101		3650
	To record payment of first and last month's rent, commission and deposits for 20 W. 36th Street building			

Figure 4.4

Cash Disbursements Journal

The cash disbursements journal is a specialized journal designed to record all cash disbursements—usually checks written. The cash disbursements journal is comparable to the check register because it records all the checks written and what accounts they represent. The cash disbursements journal differs from the check register in that it has special columns for accounts for which many checks are written. For instance, payments of accounts payable and purchases of inventory for cash might require a large number of checks to be written monthly, so the cash disbursements journal has special columns for these items.

The cash disbursements journal allows you to show on one line both the debit (to the account the check is made out to) and the credit (cash) in each transaction. The illustration following (Figure 4.5) is an example of a cash disbursements journal.

The cash disbursement journal also has a check (√) column to show when the accounts were posted to a ledger.

Cash Disbursements Journal Examples.   John Jones realizes that the business is going to be paying out a lot of checks for expenses, reducing debt and accounts payable, and making other purchases in the business. A cash disbursement journal is started so that entries may be made easier and summaries of the transactions will not have to be written every time a check is paid. Jones decides he should have special columns for accounts payable since he will require inventory purchases on credit. He thinks he will pay for some subcontract work in cash since some of the components he must use for his designs have to be custom made by small companies which will not extend credit. A column for subcontract work is included.

Example One.   John writes a check to Titan Telephone for telephone installation and deposits. It is check number 104 and it is written on January 6 for $430, $300 for installation expense and $130 as a deposit.

The original transaction documents include: a receipt from Titan Telephone, Inc., and a check from Hero Manufacturing. The cash disbursements journal entry is in Figure 4.6.

Cash Disbursements Journal for Month of Jan, 1980, page 1

Date	Check No.	Explanation	Acct. No.	Sundry Debits		Accts. Pay.		Sub-Cont. CR	Cash in Bank
				√	Amount	√	Dr. 201	600-610	CR. 101

Figure 4.5

CASH DISBURSEMENTS JOURNAL

Date	Check No.	Explanation	Acct. No.	Sundry Debits Amount	Accts. Pay. Dr. 201	Sub-Contract CR600-610	Cash in Bank CR. 101
1980							
1/6	104	Titian Telephone-installation	510	300			
		Titian Telephone - deposit	122	130			430
1/6	105	CCPSC	201.1		500		500
1/6	106	Assemblies, Inc.	601			1200	1200
1/7	107	Office Supplies	560	150			150
1/7	108	Business License	591	40			40

Figure 4.6

Telephone expense and telephone deposits are debited (increased) and cash is credited (decreased). The transaction involves both an increase (deposits) and a decrease (cash) in assets and an increase in expense.

Example Two. Hero needs to pay off some of the money that is owed to Computer and Circuit Parts Supply Company (CCPSC). John writes check 105 for $500 to CCPSC on January 6.

The original transaction document is a check from Hero. The cash disbursements journal entry is in Figure 4.6.

CCPSC accounts payable (account number 201) is debited (decreased) and cash in the bank (account 101) is credited (decreased). The transaction involves a decrease in both a liability (accounts payable) and an asset (cash).

Example Three. Hero pays Assemblies, Inc., for subcontract work performed on the Hero computer system. Hero writes check 106 for $1200.

The transaction documents include: a check from Hero and a paid receipt form Assemblies, Inc. The cash disbursements journal entry is Figure 4.6.

Subcontract expense (601) is debited (increased) and cash is credited (decreased). The transaction involves an increase in a cost of sales (subcontract) and a decrease in an asset (cash).

Example Four. Hero writes check 107 on January 7 to ABC Office Supply for $150.

The transaction documents include: a check from Hero and a sales receipt from ABC Office Supply. The cash disbursements journal entry is Figure 4.6.

Sundry debits—office supplies (560) is debited (increased) and cash is credited (decreased). The transaction involves an increase in expense (office supplies) and a decrease in an asset (cash).

Example Five. Hero pays $40 for a business license, check number 108.

The transaction documents are: a check from Hero and a receipt from the government for the license and a license. The cash disbursements journal entry is Figure 4.6.

Sundry debits—business license (591) is debited (increased) and cash is credited. The transaction involves an increase in an expense and a decrease in an asset (cash).

Note. The cash disbursements journal has columnar entries for accounts that will have many transactions (such as cash and accounts payable). Cash is credited in every entry because every time a check is written (a cash disbursement is made), cash is reduced.

The Cash Receipts Journal

Jones expects his company to have sales and he thinks that the first sales he makes will be for cash. Rather than use the general journal he decides to use a cash receipts journal. The cash receipts journal records his cash sales and can record sales from different categories in separate columns. For management reasons, Jones wants to keep track of which of his sales are for computer systems and which are for component sales, so he sets up separate columns in his cash receipts journal for these two groups of sales. An example of his cash receipts journal is Figure 4.7.

For miscellaneous income there is a sundry credits column. Since Hero does rent some of their systems, it is necessary to record this source of income under a miscellaneous (sundry) credit column.

Cash Receipts Journal Examples. The following are examples of cash receipts journal transactions.

Example One. On January 8, 1980 Hero has cash sales of $378, all of which are sales of components.

The transaction documents include: sales receipts and a deposit slip for the amount of sales deposited to Hero's bank checking account. The cash receipts journal entry is shown in Figure 4.8.

Cash Receipts Journal for Month of _____ 19 ____ Page ____

Date	Explanation	Acct. No.	Sundry Credits ✓ Amount	Accounts Receivable ✓ CR. 111	Systems Sales CR 410	Components Sales CR. 420	Cash In Bank DR. 101

Figure 4.7

Cash in the bank (101) is debited (increased) and component sales (account 420) is credited (increased). The transaction involves an incrase in both assets (cash) and income (components sales).

Example Two.   The next day, January 9, Hero has cash sales of both components ($630) and systems ($510) sales.

The original transaction documents are: the sales receipts and a deposit slip to Hero's checking account. The cash receipts journal entry is shown in Figure 4.8.

Cash in the bank is debited (increased). The total amount of sales—component sales and system sales—is credited (increased). This transaction involves an increase in cash (debit), and asset, and two income accounts—component sales and systems sales.

Example Three.   On January 10, Hero received not only cash sales from systems and components, but also rental income from a unit that was on lease to K. K. Company ($350), for total sales that day of $1506.

The original transaction documents are: the sales receipts and the rental payment receipt from K. K. Company, as well as the deposit slip to Hero's bank for the total sales. The entry is shown in Figure 4.8.

Cash in the bank is debited (increased) by $1506, the total amount of systems, component, and rental income. Component and system sales are both credited (increased) as in the previous example. Rental income, which is account number 430, is also credited (increased), but it is entered under the "sundry credits" column. The

CASH RECEIPTS JOURNAL

Date	Explanation	Acct. No.	Sundry Credits ✓ Amount	Accounts Receivable ✓ CR. 111	Systems Sales CR. 410	Components Sales CR. 420	Cash In Bank DR. 101
1980							
Jan 8	DAILY SALES					378	378
Jan 9	DAILY SALES				510	630	1140
Jan 10	DAILY SALES				340	816	
	RENTAL INCOME -K.K. CO.	430	350				1506
Jan 11	DAILY SALES					530	
	JAMES KITT			75			605
Jan 12	DAILY SALES				830	620	
	RENTAL INCOME - R.G.	430	350				1800

Figure 4.8

transaction involves an increase in the asset "cash" (debit), and an increase in the "systems sales," "component sales," and "rental income" accounts (credit).

Example Four.   On January 11, Hero received $530 in component sales and $75 in payment on a receivable from James Kitt, for a total of $605. The payment from Kitt was payment for purchases before the company officially started.

The original transaction documents include: the sales receipts for component sales, a receipt to James Kitt for payment of a receivable, and the bank deposit slip for the total. The entry is shown in Figure 4.8.

Cash in the bank is debited (increased) by the total from component sales and payment of receivables. Accounts receivable are decreased (credited) and component sales are increased (credited). The transaction involves an increase in the asset cash (debit) and in sales (credit) as well as a decrease in the asset accounts receivable (credit).

Example Five.   On January 12, Hero Manufacturing receives money for component and system sales as well as rental income.

The original transaction documents are the same as for Example Three above: deposit slip to the bank and receipts for sales and rentals. The entry is shown in Figure 4.8.

Cash in the bank is debited (increased) and sales and rental accounts are credited (increased). The transaction involves an increase both in the asset cash (debit) and in component sales, system sales, and rental income (credit).

Note.   The most active columns are the sales columns in the cash receipts journal. Remember that these are only cash sales and do not include sales made on credit (reserved for the "sales journal," discussed next). Cash receipts from whatever source (cash sales, rental income, or receipts of cash payments on accounts receivable owed) are entered in the cash receipts journal. Every entry made requires debiting cash.

Sales Journal

Because sales were going well and because of demand for his product by companies that generally pay on credit, Jones decided that his company could extend credit to good customers. This allowed customers to make purchases and pay for them within a period of 30 days. In order to keep track of his customers' purchases, Jones decided to institute a special journal called the "sales journal."

A sample sales journal is shown in Figure 4.9.

The purpose of the sales journal is to record all accounts receivable as they are created by the customer and record these sales on credit as part of the gross sales of the company.

The sales journal does not record *all* sales, *only* those on credit.

The particular format that Hero Manufacturing uses, has two separate columns for systems sales and component sales as well as a column for debits to accounts receivable.

Sales Journal Examples.   The following are some examples:

Example One.   Hero, on January 13, sells a system to James Kitt on credit.

The transaction document is a sales invoice (number 100). The entry is in Figure 4.10.

Accounts receivable is debited (increased) and systems sales is credited (increased). The transaction involves an increase in the accounts receivable asset (debit) and in component sales (credit).

Sales Journal for month of _____ 19_____ Page_____

Date	Sales Slip No.	Customer's Name	Accounts Receivable DR. 111	Systems Sales CR. 410	Components Sales CR. 420

Figure 4.9

Sales Journal

Date	Sales Slip No.	Customer's Name	Accounts Receivable DR. 111	Systems Sales CR. 410	Components Sales CR. 420
1980					
1/13	100	John Kitt	350	350	
1/14	101	Thompson Co.	160		160
	102	Rick Smith	50		50
1/15	103	Armstrong Co.	50		50
1/16	104	Zipp and Co.	1250	1250	
	105	Thompson Co.	75		75
1/17	106	Johnson Components	120		120

Figure 4.10

Example Two. In January both Thompson Company and Rick Smith are sold some components on credit.

The transaction documents are credit sales invoices (number 101). The entry is shown in Figure 4.10.

Accounts receivable are debited (increased) for both the Thompson and Smith sales. Component sales are credited (increased) by both the sales to Thompson and Smith. The transaction increases the asset accounts receivable (debit) and component sales (credit).

Example Three. On January 15 Hero sells components to Armstrong Company on credit. The original transaction document is a credit sales slip. The entry is shown in Figure 4.10.

The asset accounts receivable is debited (increased) and the income account component sales is credited (increased).

Example Four. On January 16 Hero sells a system worth $1250 to Zipp and Company and $75 more in components to Thompson Company. The transaction document is again the credit sales slip. This is illustrated in Figure 4.10.

The transaction involves debiting (increasing) accounts receivable and crediting (increasing) both the system sales and component sales accounts.

Example Five. On January 17, Hero sells Johnson Components $120 worth of components on credit. The original transaction document is the sales slip (number 106). The example is illustrated in Figure 4.10.

The transaction is an increase in both accounts receivable (debit) and component sales (credit).

Note. The journal has a place for the sales slip number which could save a lot of time when tracing it down in the future. Accounts receivable is always debited when any entry is made.

Purchases Journal

The last commonly used special journal is the purchases journal. The purchases journal is for recording purchases made on *credit only*.

An example of the purchases journal form is Figure 4.11.

Hero needs a purchases journal to keep track of the goods bought from suppliers on credit. The purchases journal is for recording Hero's accounts payable as they are incurred. The purchases journal only has entries for when the goods are purchased on credit. It does not record the payments to the suppliers on account. If Hero pays what they owe to the suppliers, the entry would appear in the cash disbursements journal.

The purchases journal has a column for the date, the name of the supplier, the number of the supplier's invoice, the date of that invoice, the terms, and a column for credits to accounts payable and debits to inventory purchases.

Purchases Journal Examples. The following are some examples:

Example One. On January 18, Hero buys some merchandise from Computer and Circuits Parts Supply Company (CCPSC) for $2000 on Credit.

The original transaction document is an invoice number 10311, dated 1/14/80 from CCPSC. The terms are 2/10 net 30. This means that if Hero pays for the merchandise in 10 days they will receive a 2% discount from the invoice amount. If Hero does not

Purchases Journal

Date	Purchased From	In. No.	In. Date	Terms	✓	Accounts Payable CR. 201	Inventory Purchases DR. 601

Figure 4.11

take advantage of this discount, they have 30 days to pay for the merchandise. This is illustrated in Figure 4.12.

The transaction involves an increase (debit) in the expense inventory purchases and an increase (credit) in the liability accounts payable.

Example Two. On January 25 Hero buys merchandise on credit from Richland Components.

The original transaction document is Richland invoice number 207, dated 1/21/80 with net 30 day terms. Richland Components does not offer a discount and their normal terms are payment due in 30 days. The example is in Figure 4.12.

The transaction, as in the case with all other examples in the purchases journal, increases inventory purchases (debit) and increases accounts payable (credit).

Example Three. On January 26, Hero buys some more merchandise on credit from CCPSC. The original transaction document is the invoice number 10410 from CCPSC. This is illustrated in Figure 4.12.

The transaction increases both inventory purchase (debit) and accounts payable (credit).

Example Four. On the 29th of January, Hero buys $500 worth of components on credit from Richland Components. The original transaction document is invoice 250 issued by Richland. The entry appears in Figures 4.12.

The transaction increases the expense inventory purchases (debit) and the liability accounts payable (credit).

Purchasers Journal

Date	Purchased From	In. No.	In. Date	Terms	Accounts Payable CR. 201	Inventory Purchases DR. 601
1980						
1/18	C C PSC	10311	1/14	2-10-30	2000	2000
1/25	Richland Components	207	1/21	N/30	1520	1520
1/26	C C PSC	10410	1/24	2-10-30	1400	1400
1/29	Richland Components	250	1/27	N/30	500	500
1/30	Top Component	816	1/29	N/30	1800	1800

Figure 4.12

Example Five. On January 30 Hero purchases $1800 worth of merchandise from Top Component, invoice number 816 with net 30 day terms. See Figure 4.12.

The transaction increases the expense inventory purchases and increases accounts payable (credit).

Note. Every transaction involves a debit to inventory purchases and a credit to accounts payable. Listing the invoice number, date, and terms will help avoid unnecessary difficulties in the future.

LEDGERS (THE SUMMARY BOOKS)

Now Hero has an ability to analyze all their accounting transactions because they have recorded them chronologically in the special journals. If they want to review the checks they have written in a given period, they analyze the cash disbursement journal. They can track their purchases, cash receipts, credit sales, and other transactions in total—and in chronological order—without examining the original checks.

But what if Hero wants to find out what their total expenditure for the last month was for merchandise from Richland Components? What if they want to find out what James Kitt bought from them during the last year, or how much they spent on utilities?

One way to find these totals is to go back through the journals for the whole period, find the separate items, and total them. Another way would be to write or call the supplier, customer, or utility company and ask them for the total. The best way, however, is to keep a summary book for the period, transferring each entry to a particular category. In other words, if you had a book that listed each account separately (a page for utilities, a page for Richland Components, etc.) you could tell at a glance how much you owe, who owes you or how much you've already paid.

A book that lists each account under a separate category is called a *ledger*.

Weekly, monthly, or quarterly, all the journals are totaled and "posted" into ledgers. Ledgers are summaries of activities under each account in the chart of accounts. They are divided into two groups: the general ledger and the subsidiary ledgers.

In the general ledger all the accounts are posted after a given period from their respective journal or journals. Entries in the journal indicate to the bookkeeper what is to be debited and what is to be credited. With the journals as a guide, the information is entered into the respective individual ledger accounts. The book-keeper uses printed forms for his account records. Each account is kept on a separate form called a ledger sheet. All the accounts taken together constitute a ledger. It becomes the master reference book of the accounting system and provides a permanent and classified record of every element involved in the business operation.

The general ledger is divided into separate accounts (e.g., "cash 101"), with a debit and credit column for each account. A look at the ledger account record will reveal a complete history of the increases and decreases of the accounts involved. Ledgers may be kept in book or card form. Or, of course, these records may be kept in computer files.

General Ledger Format

Figure 4.13 shows a general ledger format. Note that the format has a column for the date. The date used here may be either the date the entry was made in a journal or the date that the entry was transferred from the journal to the ledger. The former is preferable, but either is acceptable as long as the bookkeeper is consistent.

There are two columns for explanation and two for posting references. This allows an explanation and a posting reference for a debit and credit entry separately. The explanation is usually something like "total 1/15/78" or the name to whom a check was made payable.

The posting reference refers to the journal that is the source of the entry. Generally in the posting reference, the type of journal and the page number are given. However, in the case of the general journal, the journal entry number is used. For instance, if a total for cash disbursed (credit to cash) is taken from the cash disbursement journal at the end of the month, the post reference would be "CDJ-1," which means the entry comes from the cash disbursement journal. Summaries would have a post reference like "GJ-1-5" meaning general journal, entry 1-5, which is the fifth entry (5) for the month of January (1).

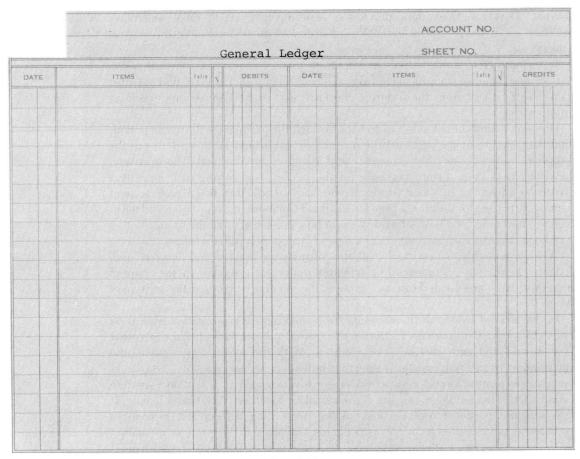

Figure 4.13

The abbreviations that are commonly used for the posting references are shown below:

Table of Journal Abbreviations

Name of journal	Abbreviations used
General journal	GJ
Cash disbursements journal	CDJ
Cash receipts journal	CRJ
Purchases journal	PJ
Sales journal	SJ

The ledger format is divided into a debit and a credit side. If the entry is a credit, it is entered on the credit side; if a debit, it is entered on the debit side.

Note also that the format has a line at the top and a space for the number of the account. These should be filled in. The accounts are usually listed in the general journal in order of their chart of account numbers. The first account entered is usually "cash" or "cash in bank," plus the account number such as "101."

Ledger Examples.   The journal entries used in the first part of this chapter for Hero Manufacturing will now be posted to the general ledger and special ledger accounts.

First the completed general ledger is shown in Figure 4.14. A discussion of each account follows.

General Comments.   *All entries* from the general journal are posted to the ledger. With the special journals such as the cash disbursements, cash receipts, sales, and purchases journals, it is different. In the special journals, the columns that have the most activity, especially those that require entries each time the journal is used, are *added* up at the end of a period and their *totals* are posted to the ledger. Each journal and the columns from each journal that are totaled at the end of the period are indicated below:

Journal	Account Columns Totaled and Posted
General Journal	None
Cash Disbursements Journal	1. Cash in bank
	2. Accounts payable
	3. All other columns except sundry debits
Cash Receipts Journal	1. Cash in bank
	2. Accounts receivable
	3. Income accounts except sundry credits
Sales Journal	1. Accounts receivable
	2. All income accounts
Purchases Journal	1. Accounts payable
	2. Inventory purchases

In the special journals, the columns that are *not* totaled are the "sundry" columns, either "sundry debits" or "sundry credits." In the general journal, no totals are obtained and each entry is posted to the ledger separately.

The traditional technique of totaling a column in a special journal is called footing. Footing is simply the process of drawing a line at the bottom of the column in pencil and writing the total under the line in pencil.

100 Accounts.   *Cash* (account number 101) in the general ledger example has the most entries from the journals (7), which is a typical situation. The first two entries on the debit side and the first three entries on the credit side came from the general journal (GJ in the post reference column). All entries from the general journal are posted to the ledger. The last entry on the debit side is the cash debit total from January 1 through January 12, 1980 from the cash receipts journal (CRJ). The last entry on the credit side is the cash credit total from the cash disbursements journal (CDJ). The total represents entries in the cash disbursements journal from January 1 through January 7.

Accounts Receivable (account number 111) has only two entries. One is a debit entry of $2055, which is the column total from the sales journal (SJ), page 1. The credit entry is $75 with the accounts receivable credit (payments) from the cash receipts journal (CRJ). Each separate customer account transaction is usually posted in a special ledger known as the accounts receivable ledger. Only the total of the accounts receivable *customer credit extended* and the payments made on these accounts are entered in the accounts receivable ledger account in the general journal. This account is sometimes called the "accounts receivable control account."

CASH   ACCOUNT NO. 101

SHEET NO. 1

DATE	ITEMS	Folio	√	DEBITS	DATE	ITEMS	Folio	√	CREDITS
1980					1980				
Jan 1	OWNER'S EQUITY	GJ1-1		25000	Jan 3	TEST EQUIPMENT	GJ1-3		5000
2	BANK LOAN	GJ1-2		25000	4	INVENTORY	GJ1-4		15000
12	TOTAL JAN 1-12	CRJ-1		5429	5	RENT/DEPOSITS	GJ1-5		3650
					7	TOTAL JAN 1-7	CDJ-1		6820

ACCOUNTS RECEIVABLE   ACCOUNT NO. 111

SHEET NO. 1

DATE	ITEMS	Folio	√	DEBITS	DATE	ITEMS	Folio	√	CREDITS
1980					1980				
Jan 17	TOTAL CREDIT SALES	SJ-1		2055	Jan 12	PAYMENTS	CRJ-1		75

PRE-PAID RENT   ACCOUNT NO. 120

SHEET NO. 1

DATE	ITEMS	Folio	√	DEBITS	DATE	ITEMS	Folio	√	CREDITS
1980									
Jan 5	RENT	GJ1-5		500					

DEPOSITS   ACCOUNT NO. 122

SHEET NO. 1

DATE	ITEMS	Folio	√	DEBITS	DATE	ITEMS	Folio	√	CREDITS
1980									
Jan 5	RENT DEPOSITS	GJ1-5		1400					
6	TITIAN TELEPHONE	CDJ-1		130					

Figure 4.14

PARTS INVENTORY — ACCOUNT NO. 130 — SHEET NO. 1

DATE	ITEMS	Folio	√	DEBITS	DATE	ITEMS	Folio	√	CREDITS
1980 Jan 4	CCPSC	GJ1-4		30000					

TEST EQUIPMENT — ACCOUNT NO. 150.1 — SHEET NO. 1

DATE	ITEMS	Folio	√	DEBITS	DATE	ITEMS	Folio	√	CREDITS
1980 Jan 3	ZARKOFF	GJ1-3		10000					

ACCOUNTS PAYABLE — ACCOUNT NO. 201 — SHEET NO. 1

DATE	ITEMS	Folio	√	DEBITS	DATE	ITEMS	Folio	√	CREDITS
1980 Jan 7	TOTAL JAN 1-7	CDJ-1		5000	1980 Jan 4	CCPSC	GJ1-4		15000
					Jan 30	TOTAL JAN 1-30	PJ-1		7220

NOTES PAYABLE - BANK OF AMERIGOLD — ACCOUNT NO. 211.1 — SHEET NO. 1

DATE	ITEMS	Folio	√	DEBITS	DATE	ITEMS	Folio	√	CREDITS
					1980 Jan 4	FIRST LOAN	GJ1-2		25000

Figure 4.14 (cont.)

NOTE PAYABLE - ZARKOFF EQUIPMENT

ACCOUNT NO. 211.2

SHEET NO. 1

DATE	ITEMS	Folio	√	DEBITS	DATE	ITEMS	Folio	√	CREDITS
					1980				
					Jan 3	INITIAL EQUIP.	GJ-3		5000

JOHN JONES EQUITY

ACCOUNT NO. 301

SHEET NO. 1

DATE	ITEMS	Folio	√	DEBITS	DATE	ITEMS	Folio	√	CREDITS
					1980				
					Jan 1	INITIAL CAPITAL	GJ-1		25000

SYSTEMS SALES

ACCOUNT NO. 410

SHEET NO. 1

DATE	ITEMS	Folio	√	DEBITS	DATE	ITEMS	Folio	√	CREDITS
					1980				
					Jan 12	TOTAL JAN 1-12	CRJ-1		1680
					17	TOTAL JAN 1-17	SJ-1		1600

COMPONENT SALES

ACCOUNT NO. 420

SHEET NO. 1

DATE	ITEMS	Folio	√	DEBITS	DATE	ITEMS	Folio	√	CREDITS
					1980				
					Jan 12	TOTAL JAN 1-12	CRJ-1		2974
					17	TOTAL JAN 1-17	SJ-1		455

Figure 4.14   (cont.)

RENTAL INCOME
ACCOUNT NO. 430
SHEET NO. 1

DATE	ITEMS	Folio	√	DEBITS	DATE		ITEMS	Folio	√	CREDITS
					1980					
					Jan	12	TOTAL JAN 1-12	CRJ-1		700

RENT EXPENSE
ACCOUNT NO. 508
SHEET NO. 1

DATE		ITEMS	Folio	√	DEBITS	DATE	ITEMS	Folio	√	CREDITS
1980										
Jan	5	FIRST MONTH RENT	GJ1-5		500					

RENTAL COMMISSION
ACCOUNT NO. 509
SHEET NO. 1

DATE		ITEMS	Folio	√	DEBITS	DATE	ITEMS	Folio	√	CREDITS
1980										
Jan	5	FINDER'S FEE	GJ1-5		1250					

TELEPHONE EXPENSE
ACCOUNT NO. 510
SHEET NO. 1

DATE		ITEMS	Folio	√	DEBITS	DATE	ITEMS	Folio	√	CREDITS
1980										
Jan	6	TITIAN TELEPHONE	CDJ-1		300					

Figure 4.14 (cont.)

OFFICE SUPPLIES — ACCOUNT NO. 560

SHEET NO. 1

DATE	ITEMS	Folio	√	DEBITS	DATE	ITEMS	Folio	√	CREDITS
1980									
Jan 7		CDJ-1		150					

BUSINESS LICENSE — ACCOUNT NO. 591

SHEET NO. 1

DATE	ITEMS	Folio	√	DEBITS	DATE	ITEMS	Folio	√	CREDITS
1980									
Jan 7		CDJ-1		40					

INVENTORY PURCHASES — ACCOUNT NO. 601

SHEET NO. 1

DATE	ITEMS	Folio	√	DEBITS	DATE	ITEMS	Folio	√	CREDITS
1980									
Jan 30	TOTAL JAN 1-30	PJ-1		7220					

SUB - CONTRACT — ACCOUNT NO. 610

SHEET NO. 1

DATE	ITEMS	Folio	√	DEBITS	DATE	ITEMS	Folio	√	CREDITS
1980									
Jan 7		CDJ-1		1200					

Figure 4.14   (cont.)

Prepaid Rent (account number 120.1) has one entry which is for the last month's rent recorded in the general journal (GJ) on January 5, 1980.

The Deposits (account number 122) has two entries, one for rent deposit from the general journal, entry 1-5 (GJ 1-5), and one for a telephone deposit from the cash disbursements journal page 1 (CDJ-1). Since deposits are an asset that represents money that will not become an expense until some time in the future, most entries are debit (increasing) entries. This is also the case with prepaid expense (like prepaid rent).

Parts Inventory (account number 130) has one entry which represents the initial inventory purchase, or beginning inventory, which is an asset. The entry comes from the general journal, entry 1-4 (GJ 1-4).

Test Equipment (account number 150.1) represents the purchase of equipment from Zarkoff, entered in the general journal (GJ 1-3). The full amount of the value (purchase price) of the equipment is entered here, not just the amount paid out in cash as a down payment.

Note on All 100 Accounts: All accounts from 100 to 199 are asset accounts. This means that generally they will have a debit balance, and the majority of the entries will be debit entries. Cash and Accounts Receivable are the only accounts that will receive frequent credit entries.

200 Accounts. *Accounts Payable* (number 201) has three entries. The only debit entry is the total of all accounts payable paid in cash for that period from the cash disbursements journal, page 1 (CDJ-1). The first entry (January 4) on the credit side of the Accounts Payable ledger is from the general journal (GJ 1-4). The second entry is the total of all the merchandise credit Hero Manufacturing received in the period from the purchases journal, page 1 (PJ-1).

Notes Payable—Bank of Amerigold (number 211.1) has one credit entry. This entry records the total amount of the loan from the general journal (GJ 1-2). Each time the company secures a loan it will be a credit entry for the total amount. This account will have debit entries for each time the principal portion of the loan is paid. Each month that a payment on the loan is made, the interest portion of that payment will be listed as interest expense, and the principal portion of the payment will be debited to this account.

Note Payable—Zarkoff Equipment (account 211.2) has one entry, the initial amount owed on the equipment purchased and recorded as an asset in account 150.1 (test equipment). This is a credit entry from the general journal (GJ 1-3). As with the Note Payable—Bank of Amerigold account above, each time the note is paid, the principal portion of that payment will be entered as a debit to this account.

Note on 200 Accounts. All 200 accounts are liability accounts. They generally have *credit* balances. Accounts payable and the notes payable accounts will, however, have frequent debit entries. The majority of the loan payable account entries will be debit entries for principal portion payment of debt.

300 Accounts. *John Jones—Equity* (account 301) has only the amount of the original equity injection as an entry. This entry is from the general journal (GJ 1-1). This account receives entries only once per period when the company calculates profit or loss or when the owner(s) inject capital. Generally, this account will have a credit balance. Debit entries are made only for losses or owner's draw. In the examples from Hero Manufacturing, this is the only equity account.

400 Accounts. *Systems Sales* (account 410) has two entries, one from the cash receipts journal (CRJ-1) representing *cash* sales, and one from the sales journal (SJ-1) representing *credit* sales. Both entries are totals added up at the end of the period.

Component Sales(account 420), like the Systems Sales Account, above, has a cash sales and a credit sales entry. Both entries are credits; the cash sales entry comes from the cash receipts journal (CRJ-1) and the credit sales entry comes from the sales journal (SJ-1). Both entries are totals from the end of the period.

Rental Income (account 430) has one entry. This entry is from the cash receipts journal, page 1 (CRJ-1) which is the total of rental income from January 1 through January 12, 1980.

Note on 400 Accounts. All 400 accounts are revenue accounts. Revenue accounts usually have a credit balance and rarely receive a debit entry. The only debit entry posted in these accounts would be for sales returns or allowances.

500 Accounts. *Rent Expense* (account 508) has a single debit entry, that from the general journal (GJ 1-5).

Rental Commission (account 509) has one entry from the general journal (GJ 1-5).

Telephone Expense (account 510) has a debit entry from the cash disbursements journal (CDJ-1) for a monthly telephone expense.

Office Supplies (account 560) has a debit entry from the cash disbursements journal dated January 7.

Business License Expense (account 591) has a debit entry for $40 from the cash disbursements journal.

Note on 500 Accounts. All 500 accounts are expense accounts. They will usually have a debit balance and will, except in rare circumstances, have only debit entries.

600 Accounts. *Inventory Purchases* (account 601) has a debit entry for the purchases of merchandise from January 1 through January 30 from the purchases journal.

Subcontract (account 610) has a debit entry from the cash disbursements journal from January 7.

Note on 600 Accounts. All 600 accounts will usually have debit balances. Almost all of the entries in these accounts will be debit entries. The 600 accounts are the cost of sales accounts and the only credit entries will be for returns of merchandise or discounts.

Special Ledgers (Accounts Receivable and Accounts Payable Ledgers)

It is important for a company to keep careful track of who owes what for product sales. You also want to know how much your customer owes you, for how long, when he bought, and how much he bought. The total in the sales journal will tell you the total sales on credit you have, and if you trace through it and separate out the customers, you can find the individual statistics. Most people, however, find that it is much easier to keep an account for each customer apart from the sales journal. The ledger that keeps track of what each customer purchases and later pays for under the customer's name is called the *accounts receivable ledger*.

The ledger that keeps track of what you owe to your suppliers under the suppliers' names is called the *accounts payable ledger*. The reasons for keeping the accounts payable ledger are the same as the reasons for keeping the accounts receivable ledger, although perhaps not as compelling. When you are continually ordering and paying for merchandise it becomes difficult to keep track of the exact balance you owe each supplier and how much you typically buy from them. This is especially true when a company has several suppliers. Although your supplier will be glad to tell you how much you owe at any given time, it is a mistake to depend on their honesty and accuracy.

Figures 4.15 and 4.16 are samples of the special ledger format. The same format is used for both the accounts receivable ledger and the accounts payable ledger.

The format has a place for the name of the account. This would be the customer's name in the accounts receivable ledger and the supplier's name in the accounts payable ledger. It also includes a space for terms, such as net 30 days, 2/10 net 30, and so on. It has a column for the date of the transactions—the date the order was shipped—from the sales journal or the purchases journal, or payments recorded in the cash receipts or the cash disbursements journal.

It also has a column for a description, which is generally information such as the invoice number. The posting reference column could be used for the name and page number of the special journals or for the general journal. This is the same column that was used before in the general ledger. An example would be "PJ-1" which means that the entry is from the purchases journal, page 1.

The debit column in the accounts receivable ledger would be for all credit sales to customers recorded in the sales journal. The credit column in the accounts receivable ledger would be used to record payments from the cash receipts journal. In the accounts payable ledger the debit column is for payments made to suppliers from the cash disbursements journal and the credit column is to record any trade credit that you receive from the suppliers recorded in the purchases journal.

The balance column is the amount now owed the supplier in the case of the accounts payable ledger or the amount the customer owes you in the case of the accounts receivable ledger.

The accounts receivable ledger generally has a *debit* balance. The accounts payable ledger generally has a *credit* balance.

Examples of Special Ledgers. The following examples are from Hero Manufacturing. The special ledgers are posted directly from the journals. The *Accounts Receivable Ledger* (Figure 4.15) shows six customers: Armstrong Company, Rick Smith, James Kitt, Johnson Components, Thompson Company and Zipp and Company. Hero Manufacturing extends 30 day terms.

Armstrong Company ordered $50 worth of merchandise on January 15. It was recorded in the sales journal, page 1 (SJ-1).

Rick Smith ordered and was delivered $50 worth of merchandise. This was recorded in the sales journal, page 1 (SJ-1).

James Kitt was delivered $75 worth or merchandise before Hero opened for business on December 12, 1979. This transaction was not recorded, the only record being a sales slip. Kitt paid off the credit on January 11 and it was recorded in the cash receipts journal (CRJ-1), bringing the balance to zero ($0). On January 13, Kitt was delivered $350 worth of merchandise, bringing the debit balance to $350.

Johnson Components purchased merchandise on January 17, recorded January 17 in the sales journal (SJ-1).

Thompson Company made two purchases from Hero, on January 14 and 16, and it has made no payments. Both purchases are from the sales journal, and the debit balance outstanding (how much they owe Hero Mfg.) is $235 as of January 16.

Zipp and Company made one purchase of $1250 on January 16, recorded in the sales journal (SJ-1).

The Accounts Payable Ledger (Figure 4.16) has three accounts for suppliers who have sold to Hero on credit: CCPSC with 2/10 net 30 terms, and Richland Components and Top Component with net 30 terms.

CCPSC is Hero's most active supplier. On January 4, Hero bought $15,000 worth of merchandise from CCPSC recorded in the General Journal (GJ-1-3). Hero paid $5000 on that amount on January 6 with check number 105, recorded in the cash disbursements journal (CDJ-1), bringing the balance owed (credit balance) down to

Armstrong Company   N 30

Date	Description	Post Ref.	Debit	Credit	Balance
1/15		SJ-1	50		50

Rick Smith   N 30

Date	Description	Post Ref.	Debit	Credit	Balance
1/14		SJ-1	50		50

James Kitt   N 30

Date	Description	Post Ref.	Debit	Credit	Balance
12/12/79	sales slip only	—	75		75
1/11/80		CRJ-1		75	—o—
1/13		SJ-1	350		350

Johnson Components   N 30

Date	Description	Post Ref.	Debit	Credit	Balance
1/17		SJ-1	120		120

Thompson Company   N 30

Date	Description	Post Ref.	Debit	Credit	Balance
1/14		SJ-1	160		160
1/16		SJ-1	75		75

Zipp and Company   N 30

Date	Description	Post Ref.	Debit	Credit	Balance
1/16		SJ-1	1250		1250

Figure 4.15

	C C P S C				2/10 N 30
Date	Description	Post Ref.	Debit	Credit	Balance
1/4/80	initial inventory	GJ1-3		15000	15000
1/6	check 105	CDJ-1	5000		10000
1/18	invoice 10311 1/14/80	PJ-1		2000	12000
1/26	invoice 10410 1/24/80	PJ-1		1400	13400

	Richland Components				N 30
Date	Description	Post Ref.	Debit	Credit	Balance
1/25/80	invoice 207 1/21/80	PJ-1		1520	1520
1/29	invoice 250 1/27/80	PJ-1		500	2020

	Top Components				N 30
Date	Description	Post Ref.	Debit	Credit	Balance
1/30/80	invoice 816 1/28/80	PJ-1		1800	1800

Figure 4.16

$10,000. Hero ordered more merchandise on January 18 and January 26, both recorded in the purchases journal (PJ-1). The January 18 purchase was CCPSC invoice number 10311, dated 1/4/80. It brought the credit balance up to $12,000 owed. The next purchase was invoice number 10410, dated 1/24/80. This brought the credit balance owed up to $13,400.

Richland Components shipped two orders of merchandise to Hero, both recorded in the purchases journal (PJ-1). The first order was received January 25, invoice number 297, dated 1/21/80. The second order, invoice number 250, was for $500 bringing the credit balance owed up to $2020.

Top Component sold $1800 worth of merchandise to Hero, invoice number 816, which was recorded in the purchases journal (PJ-1).

ACCOUNT PERIODS

An accounting period can be a maximum of one year and usually not less than one month. Large corporations which have stock traded in the public market usually end their accounting period every three months and then obtain final totals at the end of a year. Smaller businesses and closely-held corporations usually end their accounting period at the end of a year, and they total up what their transactions were for the year for income tax purposes.

At the end of a period, all of the accounts that a business has (assets, liabilities, equity, revenue, expenses) have to be totaled and summarized.

The summarizing process performed on a business's books is called "closing the books."

The Assumptions of Accounting for Business

To understand the process of "closing the books" one must understand the primary assumptions of accounting in regard to a business. These assumptions are:

1. Businesses are ongoing entities with unlimited life.
2. Although businesses have unlimited lifetimes, they require "an accounting" of their actions at least once per year.
3. There is a part of a business's accounts that lives forever and another part that "dies" each time an accounting is made. That is, there will be "permanent" and "cyclical" accounts.

First, let's discuss the proposition that a business's life is unlimited. In the early days of accounting there usually wasn't any reason for closing the books. The accountant just kept track of the transactions as they happened. Few people were interested in what the cumulative total was until the business was dissolved. Every business is expected to continue until the owner sells or retires, and it is in this spirit that the accounting records are kept.

A business may in fact exist on a moment-to-moment basis with an unpredictable future, but there is an assumption of unlimited life.

For instance, to prepare a depreciation schedule for the business and for tax purposes, an accountant must assume that the business will last long enough for the equipment to become completely "depreciated."

The second assumption, that businesses with an unlimited lifetime require periodic "accountings," is of recent origin. Historically, there was no reason to summarize the accounts at the end of a period because transactions were relatively few and simple. As the number of accounts grew, the importance of periodically summarizing the transactions became important for two reasons: (1) It provided "milestones" to compare how the business did in the past with how it is doing now. The periodic accountings (closing of the books) of a business show the business's past performance against its persent performance. (2) In most countries, a periodic accounting is required by law.

Governments require that every business prepare a summary of their business performance (sales, expenses, profit, etc.) for tax purposes. Businesses are then taxed on the basis of these "summaries." The summaries that the United States government requires of business are called "income (or profit and loss) statements" and in some cases a "statement of financial condition" (balance sheet). If the company is publicly traded it must provide annual reports and financial statements quarterly. All these "summaries" that business provides to the government are for periods no longer than one year.

The third assumption, that some accounts have only a limited (cyclical) life and others are permanent, is a result of the periodic accounting assumption. Some accounting information is only needed for a one period summary. For the next period summary, the information from the first period is not needed. For example, sales for last year are not needed to calculate this year's sales. Expenses and cost of sales incurred last year should not be added to this year's expense and cost of sales. Sales, expenses, and cost of sales records need only exist for the one period that they are used to calculate profit or loss. These are "cyclical" accounts.

Some accounts continue as the business does. These accounts are never closed, but are simply summarized and brought forward each year. These "permanent accounts" are assets, liabilities, and equity. Obviously, if you owe someone money at the end of one period (liabilities), that obligation will continue into the next period. If someone owes you money (accounts receivable—an asset), this obligation will also continue into the next year. Your company's equipment (buildings, cash, inventory, and other assets) also has a permanent nature. These assets are not lost at the end of the period. Rather, they retain their value from one period to the next.

THE TRIAL BALANCE AND THE ACCOUNTING WORKSHEET

Format of the Trial Balance

Figure 4.17 shows the format of a trial balance worksheet. Notice that the illustration has one column for the account number (usually taken in numerical order) and another column for the name of the account. The third and fourth columns are for recording the totals from each account in the general ledger.

The trial balance is made to test if the accounts properly balance. The total debits should equal the total credits. Finding the equality of debits and credits is determined by:

- Determining the total balance in each account in the General Ledger.
- Adding debit and credit balances separately to see if the totals are equal.

The balance of an account is computed by (1) adding the figures on each side, then (2) subtracting the smaller total from the larger total to obtain the difference.

Using the cash account (account number 101) of Hero Manufacturing (Figure 4.18), first the debit side is added, then we add the credit side. The total of each column is usually entered in pencil at the bottom of the column. These totals are called *footings.*

Adding up the debit column we see that the total cash taken in by the business adds up to $55,429. The total cash spent by the company in this period (cash credits) adds up to $30,470. Now, subtracting the smaller total (the credit balance of $30,470) from the larger total (the debit balance of $55,429), we get $24,959. This number is the excess of the debit column over the credit column, so therefore the account is considered to have a $24,959 *debit* balance.

As you see in the example, this $24,959 debit balance is written in pencil under the explanation column on the debit side.

No footings are required if the account only has one entry on one side or one entry on each side. The balance is simply written in the explanation space on the side (debit or credit) of the balance.

When the balances in each account are known, the bookkeeper lists the accounts in numerical order, on the trial balance. The totals from the accounts are placed in the proper column: debit balances are shown in the left column and credit balances are shown in the right column.

TRIAL BALANCE WORKSHEET

Acct. No.	Account Name	Trial Balance Debit	Credit

Figure 4.17

DATE		ITEMS	folio		DEBITS	DATE		ITEMS	folio		CREDITS
Jan	1	GJ 1-1			25000	Jan	3	GJ 1-3			5000
	2	GJ 1-2			25000		4	GJ 1-4			15000
	12	CRJ-1			5429		5	GJ 1-5			3650
					55429		7	CDJ-1			6820
		BALANCE $24,959									30470

CASH ACCOUNT NO. 101 SHEET NO. 1

Figure 4.18

As an example, let's use the accounts from the general ledger illustrations and fill out a trial balance (Figure 4.19 on the following page).

Note that the 100, 500, and 600 accounts (assets, expenses, and cost of sales) are all entered in the debit column because they all have debit balances. The 200, 300, and 400 accounts (liabilities, capital, and sales) are all entered in the credit columns because they all have credit balances.

The total of the debit column is $79,629. The total of the credit column is also $79,629 and thus both columns balance. This provides evidence that the original journal entries were made correctly.

If the debit and credit columns do not equal each other, an error has been made. Some common errors are:

1. Errors in addition.
2. Recording only half an entry (the credit without the debit, or vice versa).
3. Recording both halves of the entry on the same side (two debit or two credit entries rather than one debit and one credit).
4. Recording one or more accounts incorrectly.
5. Arithmetic errors in the journal entry.
6. Arithmetic errors in balancing the accounts.
7. Errors made by putting an entry in the wrong account.

One technique used by long-time bookkeepers to find out where errors have occurred is to divide the difference between the debit side and the credit side by nine (9). If the amount of the difference is evenly divisible by nine, the discrepancy may either by a transposition ($432 for $423) or a slide ($423 for $42.30). Dividing the difference by two (2) may suggest the amount of a credit posted as a debit or vice versa.

After we have posted the trial balance and it is accurate, we can change the trial balance summary into the more usable form of an income statement and a balance sheet.

Acct. No.	ACCOUNT NAME	TRIAL BALANCE	
		DEBIT	CREDIT
101	CASH	24959	
111	ACCOUNTS RECEIVABLE	1980	
120	PREPAID RENT	500	
122	DEPOSITS	1530	
130	PARTS INVENTORY	30000	
150.1	TEST EQUIPMENT	10000	
201	ACCOUNTS PAYABLE		17220
211.1	NOTES PAYABLE - B. AMERIGOLD		25000
211.2	NOTES PAYABLE - ZARKOFF		5000
301	OWNER'S EQUITY		25000
410	SYSTEM INCOME		3280
420	COMPONENT INCOME		3429
430	RENTAL INCOME		700
508	RENTAL EXPENSE	500	
509	RENTAL COMMISSION	1250	
510	TELEPHONE EXPENSE	300	
560	OFFICE SUPPLIES	150	
591	BUSINESS LICENSE	40	
601	INVENTORY PURCHASES	7220	
610	SUB-CONTRACT	1200	
	TOTAL	79629	79629

Figure 4.19

THE INCOME STATEMENT AND BALANCE SHEET WORKPAPER FORMAT

The trial balance extended for four more columns becomes the total workpaper. Notice in Figure 4.20 that debit and credit columns are added both for the income statement and for the balance sheet.

The columns marked "income statement" and "balance sheet" are used to organize the figures needed for these financial reports. Each of these headings has two columns—one for debits and one for credits.

Accounts 100, 200 and 300 (the asset, liability, and equity accounts) are carried over to the balance sheet column. Accounts 400, 500, and 600 (the income, expense and cost of sales accounts) are carried over to the income statement columns. Accounts that had *debit* amounts in the trial balance will continue to be recorded as *debits* when transferred to the income statement. Credits from the trial balance will continue to be listed as credits in either the balance sheet or the income statement column.

Acct. No.	Account Name	Trial Balance		Income Statement		Balance Sheet	
		Debit	Credit	Debit	Credit	Debit	Credit

Figure 4.20

Figure 4.21 (on the following page) shows the trail balance expanded into the balance sheet and income statement columns.

Income Statement

The three income accounts [system sales (508), component sales (509), and rental income (510)] are moved to the credit side of the income statement. All the expense accounts are moved to the debit side of the income statement. This includes rental expense, rental commission, telephone expense, office supplies, and business licenses. All of the cost of sales accounts—inventory purchases (601) and subcontract work (610)—are moved to the debit side of the income statement.

As the next step, the bookkeeper totals both columns (debit and credit). You will notice from the example that the income statement totals do not balance. The total of the credit column (which is only the total of sales) is $7409, $3251 less than the debit total. The debit side total of the income statement is $10,660. This means that the expense and cost of sales exceeded the sales. That is, the company has a net operating loss. Since expense and cost of sales (the debit side) exceeded sales (the credit side) the company has a net loss for the difference (a $3251 loss).

This is somewhat misleading. The company may have some of the inventory it purchased left over, total expense does not include depreciation, and no allowance was made for bad debts. These are "adjustments" that will be discussed later in this chapter.

EXHIBIT 5.22 — WORK SHEET

	ACCOUNT NAME	TRIAL BALANCE		INCOME STATEMENT		BALANCE SHEET	
		DEBIT	CREDIT	DEBIT	CREDIT	DEBIT	CREDIT
101	CASH	24959				24959	
111	ACCOUNTS RECEIVABLE	1980				1980	
120	PREPAID RENT	500				500	
122	DEPOSITS	1530				1530	
130	PARTS INVENTORY	30000				30000	
150.1	TEST EQUIPMENT	10000				10000	
201	ACCOUNTS PAYABLE		17220				17220
211.1	NOTES PAYABLE - B. AMERIGOLD		25000				25000
211.2	NOTES PAYABLE - ZARKOFF		5000				5000
301	OWNER'S EQUITY		25000				25000
410	SYSTEM SALES		3280		3280		
420	COMPONENT SALES		3429		3429		
430	RENTAL INCOME		700		700		
508	RENTAL EXPENSE	500		500			
509	RENTAL COMMISSION	1250		1250			
510	TELEPHONE	300		300			
560	OFFICE SUPPLIES	150		150			
591	BUSINESS LICENSE	40		40			
601	INVENTORY PURCHASES	7220		7220			
610	SUB-CONTRACT	1200		1200			
	TOTALS	79629	79629	10660	7409	68969	72220
	NET LOSS				3251		⟨3251⟩
				10660	10660	68969	68969

Figure 4.21

Balance Sheet

All assets from the trial balance are transferred from the trial balance debit column to the balance sheet debit column. These assets include: cash (100), accounts receivable (111), prepaid rent (120), deposits (122), parts inventory (130), and test equipment (150.1). All liabilities and equity accounts are transferred from the credit column of the trial balance to the credit column of the balance sheet. The liabilities that are transferred are accounts payable (201), notes payable—Bank of Amerigold (211.1), and notes payable—Zarkoff Equipment (211.2). There is only one equity account—owner's equity—and that is transferred to the balance sheet credit column.

If you add up the debit column and the credit column of the balance sheet workpaper, you see that the liability and capital column (credit), exceeds the asset (debit) column. This is because there was a net loss of $3251 which will be deducted from the company equity ($25,000) to make the balance sheet balance. If the company had a profit, the two columns would also have different totals, but the asset column would be a larger number. Equity would have to be increased by the amount of the net profit to bring the totals into balance.

In the case of the example, the balance sheet debit (asset) total is $68,969 and the credit column (liabilities and equity) total is $72,220. Subtract the amount of the net loss carried from the income statement ($3251) from the credit side, and the totals come into balance at $68,969 each.

Again, this is not totally accurate. The ending inventory might be higher or lower than the beginning inventory (the $30,000 that Hero Manufacturing started with) and equipment should be depreciated.

ADJUSTMENTS TO ACCOUNTS

Before you add up the accounts and summarize them, there are some expenses that have to be calculated that only occur at the end of an accounting period. Depreciation and bad debt expense must be calculated. Furthermore, in all businesses which do not have a "perpetual" inventory system, a physical count of inventory must be made.

At the end of the period, the following is usually true:

1. Equipment and fixtures are carried in their accounts at their original cost without regard for the usual wear and tear during the period.
2. The amount in the accounts receivable account might include some receivable that will not be collected in the future.
3. There is no recognition of merchandise that has not been sold by the end of the period.

Depreciation

Note the adjustments format in Figure 4.22. Two adjustments columns are added to the trial balance format. Looking at Figure 4.14, the general ledger of Hero Manufacturing, we see that the company has $10,000 worth of test equipment (account 150.1).

In reality, of course, this test equipment experiences wear and tear. Accounting logic and the tax authorities allow this wear and tear to be taken into consideration and listed as an expense. This expense is called "depreciation." Depreciation is unusual in that it is not a cash expense. It is an allowance for the decline in value of the equipment.

Because most equipment does not lose all of its value in one period, the loss in value is apportioned over a longer period—the useful life of the asset. The useful life of an asset (equipment) is a period of years after which the asset will be useless to the company and, therefore, sold. The IRS has certain guidelines for different types of equipment and other assets. Generally, auto equipment is depreciated between three and five years, other types of equipment average about five to seven years useful life, and buildings and improvements have a useful life of between 15 and 20 years.

In addition to a life of five years, Hero's test equipment will also have a value at the end of that five years. This is the value that the equipment will bring if it is sold. It is called the "salvage value." Assume that in seven years the test equipment will be worthless except for the sales value of the parts. This salvage value is about $500.

The depreciation is calculated as follows:

$$\text{Equipment} - \text{Salvage Value} = \text{Depreciable Value}$$
$$\$10,000 \qquad\quad \$500 \qquad\qquad \$9500$$

$$\frac{\text{Depreciable value}}{\text{Useful life in years}} = \text{Depreciation expense each year}$$

$$\frac{\$9500}{5} = \$1900$$

Figure 4.22

When the period for which the books are being closed is less than one year, the depreciation expense must be adjusted to reflect depreciation for a period less than a year. In the example, the books are being closed for a one month period, therefore the amount of depreciation for the year ($1900) must be divided by 12. The general formula would be as follows:

$$\frac{\text{Total depreciation for year}}{\text{Number of periods in the year}} = \text{Depreciation for that period}$$

$$\frac{\$1,900}{12} = \$158.33$$

If the period were three months (one quarter) the total depreciation would be divided by four (the number of three month periods in a year).

When depreciation is calculated, it is put in an adjustments column that is alongside the trial balance columns. Depreciation is entered in the adjustments column (Figure 4.23) as a debit to depreciation expense (595) and a credit to allowance for depreciation (150.1A).

Note that in the example both entries are labeled "(A)" so that they can be easily identified for future reference.

Bad Debt Expense

In any business there is always the probability that some account receivables will not be collected.

There are two methods for determining bad debt loss. One method is to wait until the company is sure that the account of a specific customer is uncollectable, and then record the expense. An entry is made debiting a bad debt expense account and crediting the asset account, accounts receivable.

Another way to allow for this bad debt expense is to anticipate bad debt losses and provide for them ahead of time. This is called setting up an allowance for bad debts.

Bad debt losses are estimated as a percentage of total credit sales. In some industries bad debt loss might be 10% and in others it might run 1% of credit sales.

Using the industry experience, if you are a new business, or past experience if you have been in business for some time, you can set up a bad debt account.

We can calculate what the bad debt allowance should be. The industry generally experiences 3% loss on credit sales so we'll use that figure:

Credit sales for the month	$2055.00
Less: Sales returns and allowances	-0-
Net credit sales	$2055.00
Times: Estimated percentage bad debt loss	× .03
Estimated bad debts on January sales	$ 61.65

The expected bad debt loss for January sales is $61.65, 3% of total credit sales ($2055).

In Figure 4.23 bad debt allowance and expense is added to the adjustments column. The amount of bad debt for that month is debited to bad debt expense (599)

YOUR COMPANY WORK SHEET
MONTH ENDED JANUARY 1980

Acct. No.	ACCOUNT NAME	TRIAL BALANCE DEBIT	TRIAL BALANCE CREDIT	ADJUSTMENTS DEBIT	ADJUSTMENTS CREDIT	ADJUSTED TRIAL BALANCE DEBIT	ADJUSTED TRIAL BALANCE CREDIT	INCOME STATEMENT DEBIT	INCOME STATEMENT CREDIT	BALANCE SHEET DEBIT	BALANCE SHEET CREDIT
101	CASH	24959				24959					
111	ACCOUNTS RECEIVABLE	1980				1980					
111A	ALLOWANCE FOR BAD DEBT				(B)6165		6165				
120	PREPAID RENT	500				500					
122	DEPOSITS	1530				1530					
130	PARTS INVENTORY	30000				30000					
150.1	TEST EQUIPMENT	10000				10000					
150.1A	ALLOWANCE FOR DEPRECIATION				(A) 15833		15833				
201	ACCOUNTS PAYABLE		17220				17220				
211.1	NOTES PAYABLE - B.AMERIGOLD		25000				25000				
211.2	NOTES PAYABLE - ZARKOFF		5000				5000				
301	OWNER'S EQUITY		25000				25000				
410	SYSTEM SALES		3280				3280				
420	COMPONENT SALES		3429				3429				
430	RENTAL INCOME		700				700				
508	RENTAL EXPENSE	500				500					
509	RENTAL COMMISSION	1250				1250					
510	TELEPHONE	300				300					
560	OFFICE SUPPLIES	150				150					
591	BUSINESS LICENSE	40				40					
595	DEPRECIATION EXPENSE			(A) 15833		15833					
599	BAD DEBT EXPENSE			(B) 6165		6165					
601	INVENTORY PURCHASES	7220				7220					
610	SUB-CONTRACT	1200				1200					
	TOTALS	79629	79629	21998	21998	7984898	7984898				
	NET PROFIT FOR MONTH										
	TOTAL										

Figure 4.23

and credited to allowance for bad debts (111A). The allowance for bad debt (111A) is a reduction in accounts receivable expected.

Note that the two entries are marked with a "(B)" for later identification.

At this point, all the adjustments for the adjustments column next to the trial balance columns have been made. We can now total the columns. Next we add three more sets of columns: the adjusted trial balance, income statement, and balance sheet. The adjusted trial balance columns can now be filled out by adding the debit and credit columns of the trial balance with the adjustments. All the entries of the trial balance are now combined with the entries from adjustments.

There is still one more adjustment to be made to the working papers, but this will be made when the worksheet is extended to an income statement and balance sheet. The adjustment that will have to be made is in the inventory asset and the cost of sales figure.

INVENTORY AND COST OF SALES ADJUSTMENTS

Before finishing the worksheet, the accountant must recognize that some of the purchased merchandise has not yet been sold and is still on hand. For this reason the following steps must be taken: (1) The value of the merchandise that is unsold at the end of the period must be recorded as an addition to the asset inventory. (2) The cost of the merchandise sold should be recorded as part of the cost of sales.

Before any recording can be done, the company must first determine how much inventory it has on hand at the end of the period. That is, an inventory must be taken. This requires a physical count of the inventory. The result of this count is recorded on an "inventory sheet" that shows the type of item (description), the amount of that item (quantity), the unit cost, and the total.

The amount of the inventory still remaining is determined by the following computations:

Total merchandise purchases (601)	$7220.00
Less: Purchase returns and allowances	-0-
Plus: Subcontract work (610)	1200.00
Net purchases and subcontract	$8420.00
Less: Ending inventory—beginning inventory	4620.00*
Cost of goods sold	$3800.00

*Note that the beginning inventory ($30,000 used as initial inventory) has to be subtracted from the ending inventory ($34,620) to give the amount of inventory left over from the amount purchased during *that period* (January 1980). In other words, the company started with $30,000 in inventory and during the month of January bought $7220.00 worth of merchandise (not counting subcontract work). At the end of the month there was $34,620 in inventory on the premises. In order to determine how much was *purchased* during the one month period but *not sold* during that period, it is necessary to subtract out the beginning inventory ($30,000). If you subtract out the amount of inventory that you had when you started from the amount you have now, the amount that is left over ($4620.00) will be what was purchased but not sold during the period. That is, $4620 was the amount added to the existing inventory during the one month period.

Recording Inventory Adjustments on the Worksheet

The adjustments to inventory are recorded directly on the income statement and balance sheet areas of the worksheet (see Figure 4.24). The value of the closing inventory ($34,620 in the example) is recorded on the inventory line in the *debit* column of the balance sheet. The entry is marked "(C)" for identification.

The other part of the entry is a little more difficult to see. It will be a *credit* entry of $34,620 (the amount of the ending inventory) to the income statement. Also the beginning inventory of $30,000 is entered, but as a debit to the income statement. These entries will have the effect of reducing the cost of sales by the amount of inventory that was not sold. There is already an entry for the amount of inventory purchased (inventory purchases—601) of $9220. The credit entry of $34,620 and debit entry of $30,000 will reduce the effective cost of merchandise sold. This is also marked with a "(C)" for identification.

The entry of the inventory purchased but not sold in the credit column has the same effect as the cost of goods sold calculation:

Merchandise purchases (601)	$ 7,220
Plus: Subcontract (610)	1,200
Beginning inventory (120)	30,000
Less: Ending inventory	34,620
Cost of goods sold	$ 3,800

COMPLETING THE WORKSHEET

The following steps are now taken to complete the worksheet (see Figure 4.25):

1. Carry over the balances from assets, liabilities, and, equity (100, 200, and 300 accounts) to the balance sheet.
2. Carry over the balances from income, expenses, and cost of sales (accounts 400, 500, and 600) to the income statement.
3. Add up all the columns.

The income statement and the balance sheet will have different amounts in the debit and in the credit column. This difference represents the net profit. On the income statement the debit column (expenses and cost of sales) adds up to $40,879.98 and the credit column (income and inventory adjustments to cost of sales) adds up to $42,029. The difference between $42,029 (the credit total) and $40,879.98 (the debit total) is $1149.02. This amount represents the *net profit* and is added to the debit side to bring the columns in balance. Similarly, the balance sheet debit and credit columns do not balance when they are first added up, but if the $1149.02 net profit from the income statement is carried over and entered in the credit column, the totals will both add up to $73,589. This is because net profit is actually an addition to owner's equity.

YOUR COMPANY WORKSHEET
MONTH ENDED JANUARY 1980

Acct. No.	Account Name	Trial Balance Debit	Trial Balance Credit	Adjustments Debit	Adjustments Credit	Adjusted Trial Balance Debit	Adjusted Trial Balance Credit	Income Statement Debit	Income Statement Credit	Balance Sheet Debit	Balance Sheet Credit
101	CASH	24959				24959					
111	ACCOUNTS RECEIVABLE	1980				1980					
111A	ALLOWANCE FOR BAD DEBT				(B) 6165		6165				
120	PREPAID RENT	500				500					
122	DEPOSITS	1530				1530			(c)34620	(c)34620	
130	PARTS INVENTORY	30000				30000					
150.1	TEST EQUIPMENT	10000				10000					
150.1A	ALLOWANCE FOR DEPRECIATION				(A) 15833		15833				
201	ACCOUNTS PAYABLE		17220				17220				
211.1	NOTES PAYABLE - B.AMERIGOLD		25000				25000				
211.2	NOTES PAYABLE - ZARKOFF		5000				5000				
301	OWNER'S EQUITY		25000				25000				
410	SYSTEM SALES		3280				3280				
420	COMPONENT SALES		3429				3429				
430	RENTAL INCOME		700				700				
508	RENTAL EXPENSE	500				500					
509	RENTAL COMMISSION	1250				1250					
510	TELEPHONE	300				300					
560	OFFICE SUPPLIES	150				150					
591	BUSINESS LICENSE	40				40					
595	DEPRECIATION EXPENSE			(A) 15833		15833					
599	BAD DEBT EXPENSE			(B) 6165		6165					
601	INVENTORY PURCHASES	7220				7220					
610	SUB-CONTRACT	1200				1200					
	TOTALS	79629	79629	21998	21998	7984898	7984898				
	NET PROFIT FOR MONTH										
	TOTAL										

Figure 4.24

YOUR COMPANY WORKSHEET
MONTH ENDED JANUARY 1980

Acct. No.	ACCOUNT NAME	TRIAL BALANCE DEBIT	TRIAL BALANCE CREDIT	ADJUSTMENTS DEBIT	ADJUSTMENTS CREDIT	ADJUSTED TRIAL BALANCE DEBIT	ADJUSTED TRIAL BALANCE CREDIT	INCOME STATEMENT DEBIT	INCOME STATEMENT CREDIT	BALANCE SHEET DEBIT	BALANCE SHEET CREDIT
101	CASH	24959				24959				24959	
111	ACCOUNTS RECEIVABLE	1980				1980				1980	
111A	ALLOWANCE FOR BAD DEBT				(B) 6165		6165				6165
120	PREPAID RENT	500				500				500	
122	DEPOSITS	1530				1530				1530	
130	PARTS INVENTORY	30000				30000		30000	(c)34620	(c)34620	
150.1	TEST EQUIPMENT	10000				10000				10000	
150.1A	ALLOWANCE FOR DEPRECIATION				(A) 15833		15833				15833
201	ACCOUNTS PAYABLE		17220				17220				17220
211.1	NOTES PAYABLE - B. AMERIGOLD		25000				25000				25000
211.2	NOTES PAYABLE - ZARKOFF		5000				5000				5000
301	OWNER'S EQUITY		25000				25000				25000
410	SYSTEM SALES		3280				3280		3280		
420	COMPONENT SALES		3429				3429		3429		
430	RENTAL INCOME		700				700		700		
508	RENTAL EXPENSE	500				500		500			
509	RENTAL COMMISSION	1250				1250		1250			
510	TELEPHONE	300				300		300			
560	OFFICE SUPPLIES	150				150		150			
591	BUSINESS LICENSE	40				40		40			
595	DEPRECIATION EXPENSE			(A) 15833		15833		15833			
599	BAD DEBT EXPENSE			(B) 6165		6165		6165			
601	INVENTORY PURCHASES	7220				7220		7220			
610	SUB-CONTRACT	1200				1200		1200			
	TOTALS	79629	79629	21998	21998	7984898	7984898	4087998	42029	7243998	7243998
	NET PROFIT FOR MONTH							11902			11902
	TOTAL							42029	42029	73589	73589

Figure 4.25

80

INCOME STATEMENT AND BALANCE SHEET

From the worksheet, the income statement and balance sheet columns can be put into a finalized format.

To create the *income statement* (Figure 4.26) the income accounts, cost of sales accounts, expense accounts and inventory adjustments are transferred from the worksheet. Note that the cost of sales are entered as:

Beginning inventory	$30,000
Plus: Inventory purchases	7,220
Subcontract	1,220
Less: Ending inventory	34,620
Cost of goods sold	$ 3,800

Note in the example that a line for gross profit has been added which is income minus cost of goods sold and net profit which is gross profit minus operating expense.

To create the balance sheet (Figure 4.27), the asset, liability, and equity accounts from the worksheet are used. The assets are on one side of the sheet of paper and the liabilities and owner's equity are on the other side. The equation is represented as such:

$$Assets = Liabilities + Equity$$

Note that in the equity section of the balance sheet the net profit is added to the owner's original equity which equals the new owner's equity. Also note that the

HERO MANUFACTURING
INCOME STATEMENT
MONTH ENDED JANUARY, 1980

Income:		
Systems sales	$ 3,280.00	
Component sales	3,429.00	
Rental income	700.00	
Total income		$7,409.00
Less: Cost of goods sold		
Beginning inventory 1/1/80	30,000.00	
Inventory purchases	7,220.00	
Subcontract	1,200.00	
Less: Ending inventory 1/31/80	34,620.00	
Total cost of goods sold		3,800.00
Gross profit		$3,609.00
Operating expense		
Rental expense	500.00	
Rental commission	1,250.00	
Telephone	300.00	
Office supplies	150.00	
Business license	40.00	
Depreciation expense	158.33	
Bad debt expense	61.65	
Total operating expense		$2,459.98
Net profit		$1,149.02

Figure 4.26   Income Statement.

**HERO MANUFACTURING
BALANCE SHEET
JANUARY 31, 1980**

Assets		
Current assets:		
Cash	$24,959.00	
Accounts receivable	1,980.00	
Less: Bad debt	61.65	
Prepaid rent	500.00	
Deposits	1,530.00	
Parts inventory	34,620.00	
Total current assets		$63,527.35
Fixed assets:		
Test equipment	10,000.00	
Depreciation	($158.33)	
Total fixed assets		9,841.67
Total Assets		$73,369.02
Liabilities		
Current liabilities:		
Accounts payable	17,220.00	
Notes payable, BA	7,409.00	
Notes payable, ZE	2,281.00	
Total current liabilities		$26,910.00
Long-term liabilities		
Notes payable-BA	17,591.00	
Notes payable-ZE	2,719.00	
Total long-term liabilities		20,310.00
Total liabilities		$47,220.00
Equity		
Owner's capital	$25,000.00	
Net profit	1,149.02	
Total equity		26,149.02
Total liabilities		
and equity		$73,369.02

Figure 4.27   Balance sheet.

allowance for bad debt (111A) is used to reduce the accounts receivable (111), and the allowance for depreciation (150.1A) is used to reduce the value of the test equipment (150.1).

Parts inventory (130) is now the amount of the ending inventory $34,620.

Note especially that the long-term debt of notes payable—Bank of Amerigold (211.1) and notes payable—Zarkoff Equipment (211.2) have been converted into a current portion and a long-term portion. The $25,000 note to Bank of Amerigold is for three years at 12% per annum. It is paid off at $10,409 per year, $3000 of which is interest and $7409 principal. The $5000 equipment note to Zarkoff Equipment is for two years at 10% per annum simple interest. It is paid off at $2781 per year—$500 is interest and $2281 is principal. *The current portion of a long term debt is equal to the principal payment for that year.* Therefore, the current portion of the Bank of Amerigold note (211.1) is $7409 and the current portion of the Zarkoff Equipment note (211.2) is $2281.

The long-term portion is that which is not paid during the next year. Therefore, the long-term portion of the Bank of Amerigold note would be the total amount of the note ($25,000) minus the portion that will be due this year ($7409), or $17,591. Similarly the long-term portion of the Zarkoff Equipment note is the total amount of the loan ($5000) minus the current portion ($2281), or $2719.

ADJUSTING AND CLOSING ENTRIES

After the worksheet has been prepared, the last task of the bookkeeper is to make end-of-period adjustments so that the ledger accounts will agree with the worksheet and the financial statements.

The first adjustment is to record in the general journal the depreciation expense that has been calculated. Then the bad debt entry is made in the general journal. The adjustments are then posted in the general ledger accounts (see Figure 4.28).

Date	Description of Entry	Acct. No.	Debit	Credit
1980				
	1 - 6 A			
Jan 31	Depreciation Expense	595	158 33	
	Allowance for Depreciation	150.1A		158 33
	To record depreciation of test equipment for the month of January			
	1 - 7 A			
Jan 31	Bad Debt Expense	599	61 65	
	Allowance for Bad Debt	111A		61 65
	To record provision for estimated bad debt			

Figure 4.28

DATE		DESCRIPTION OF ENTRY	ACCT. NO.	✓	DEBIT	CREDIT
1980		1 – 8c				
Jan	31	PARTS INVENTORY	130		34620	
		SYSTEM SALES	410		3280	
		COMPONENT SALES	420		3429	
		RENTAL INCOME	430		700	
		INCOME AND EXPENSE SUMMARY	350			42029 00
		TO RECORD ENDING INVENTORY AND TRANSFER OF INCOME TO THE SUMMARY ACCOUNT				
		1 – 9c				
Jan	31	INCOME AND EXPENSE SUMMARY	350		40879 98	
		PARTS INVENTORY	130			30000
		RENTAL EXPENSE	508			500
		RENTAL COMMISSION	509			1250
		TELEPHONE	510			300
		OFFICE SUPPLIES	560			150
		BUSINESS LICENSE	591			40
		DEPRECIATION EXPENSE	595			158 33
		BAD DEBT EXPENSE	599			61 65
		INVENTORY PURCHASES	601			7220
		SUB-CONTRACT	610			1200
		TO TRANSFER EXPENSE, COST OF SALES AND OTHER DEBIT ITEMS TO SUMMARY ACCOUNT				

Figure 4.29

Closing Entries

After the adjustments are entered in the general ledger and general journal, the closing process begins. The procedure is as follows:

1. Transfer all account totals from the *credit* column of the income statement section of the worksheet to the income and expense summary account. Note that all the *credit* entries from the income statement become *debit* entries when they are placed in the journal.

2. Transfer the balances in the debit column of the income statement section to the income and expense summary. Note that the *debit* entries from the income statement become *credit* entries in the journal.

3. These entries that are posted in the general journal must now be transferred to the general ledger. Notice that when these entries are made all the accounts (except inventory and income and expense summary) will have a zero balance because this adjusting entry is equal to, and on the opposite side of, the total in that account. This effectively "closes" these accounts for that period, bringing their account balance to zero (see Figure 4.29).

4. Next, in the case of a proprietorship or a partnership, the accountant transfers the business profit (or loss) to the owner's drawing account. The drawing account is the account that the owner uses as his salary. It is usually referred to as "owner's draw." If the company is a corporation, the owner's salary would be an expense.

   When the drawing account is not used, the profit or loss is closed directly from the income and expense summary account to the owner's equity account. When a drawing account is used, the income and expense summary is closed directly to the drawing account.

   If John Jones, owner of Hero, decides that he wants a draw this would be reflected as a journal entry into the cash disbursements journal (he writes a check to himself) for the amount. Then the amount that he removes as draw will be posted as a *debit* entry in the drawing ledger account, decreasing the profit amount (see Figure 4.30).

5. The final procedure is to transfer the drawing account balance of $1149.02 (which would only be $649.02 if he had decided to take a $500 draw) to the equity account. This is because net profit after draw and other expenses *increases* the owner's equity. If Hero had suffered a loss in this period, the Equity account would be *decreased* by the loss.

DATE	DESCRIPTION OF ENTRY	ACCT. NO.	✓	DEBIT	CREDIT
1980	1 - 10C				
Jan 31	INCOME AND EXPENSE SUMMARY	350		1149 02	
	OWNER'S DRAWING	310			1149 02
	TO CLOSE INCOME AND EXPENSE				
	SUMMARY BY TRANSFERING				
	PROFIT TO DRAWING ACCOUNT				
	1 - 11C				
Jan 31	OWNER'S DRAWING	310		1149 02	
	OWNER'S EQUITY	301			1149 02
	TO CLOSE DRAWING ACCOUNT				
	TO EQUITY				

Figure 4.30

Summary of Closing Procedure

Step	Action
1	Total debit and credit balances in all accounts
2	Enter account balances in trial balances
3	Adjust for depreciation and bad debt on adjusted trial balance
4	Extend trial balance figures to adjusted trial balance
5	Make inventory adjustments to income statement and balance sheet columns of worksheet
6	Extend totals from adjusted trial balance columns to income statement and balance sheet columns
7	Make all closing entries in general journal and ledgers

Chapter Five

Assets

In this chapter and in Chapter 6 we will discuss assets. In a previous chapter, assets were defined as "property that is used in a trade or business." Assets contribute towards earning the income of the business, whether directly or indirectly.

Assets are productive items which contribute to income and are, generally speaking, tangible property, cash, or promises of future receipt of cash (such as accounts receivable, or investments in the business that are not considered to be an expense).

Assets include the following items (accounts):

- Cash
- Accounts receivable
- Inventory
- Investments
- Prepaid expense (such as last month's rent or utility deposits)
- Equipment
- Motor vehicles
- Furniture and fixtures
- Land and buildings
- Building improvements (called leasehold improvements if you are a renter)
- Other tangible property
- Goodwill
- Patents and copyrights
- Organizational expense

All these items can be divided into three categories: current, fixed, and other assets.

Current assets are those items that can be readily converted into cash within a one year period. Current assets are assets in which the flow of funds is one of continuous circulation or turnover in the short run.

Fixed assets are items of property, plant, and equipment and are referred to as "fixed" because of their permanent nature and because they are not subject to rapid turnover. Fixed assets are used in connection with producing or earning revenue and are not for sale in the ordinary course of business.

Other assets are all the assets that are not current and cannot fit into the fixed asset category (such as research and development, or goodwill).

CURRENT ASSETS

Current assets include cash, accounts receivable, inventory, investments (short-term), and prepaid expenses. The more important current assets are cash, accounts receivable, and inventory. Each of these will be discussed in turn.

Cash

The cash account is the most active of all business accounts. Receipts from sales (either in cash or payment of accounts receivable), receipts from the sale of assets, receipts from capital investment of the owners, and receipts of loan proceeds all go through the cash account. Disbursement for payment of expenses, cost of goods sold, repayment of a liability, payment of dividends or owner's draw, and the purchase of assets all go through the cash account. The cash account is the only account that is used in transactions with all the other groups of accounts: assets, liabilities, capital, cost of goods sold, income, and expenses.

Cash transactions in the cash account can be roughly divided into cash receipts and payments, and cash documentation in original vouchers, journals, and ledgers. Cash receipts are cash received by the company either as a result of sales of products or assets, or investment in the business, or proceeds from borrowing. Cash documentation involves the bookkeeping system of the company from the original transaction document (such as a sales receipt), to the journals (cash receipts journal), to the ledgers.

Cash Receipts and Payments. The principal cash events and their related original transaction documents are shown in Figure 5.1.

These original transaction documents initiate the processing of cash data. A cash receipt document indicates that the firm has received cash; a check indicates that a payment has been made; an adjustment advice informs the bookkeeper to record bank charges in an effort to reconcile a cash account with its related bank statement, and so on.

Event	Original Transaction Document (See Chapter 3 for Examples)
Cash is received	1. Receipt (sales receipt, check cash)
	2. Draft (bank deposit slip)
Cash is relocated or transferred	3. Deposit slip (relocation of cash to a bank account)
	4. Transfer (relocation of cash from one business or division to another, or from one bank account to another)
Cash is disbursed	5. Bank adjustment (reduction from bank account for bank service charges and adjustments)
	6. Petty cash fund
	7. Check or money order

Figure 5.1

The concept of cash receipt, relocation, and disbursement can be further illustrated in terms of how it affects journal entries as follows (see Figure 5.2).

Receipts.

1. From customers—that is, collections of accounts receivable or notes payable.
2. From cash sales.

Event/Voucher	Notation	Accounts	Debit $	Credit $
Cash is received:				
Receipt voucher	Cash provided as equity from owners	Cash Equity	5,000	5,000
	Cash provided by long-term creditors	Cash Long-term Liability	2,500	2,500
	Customer pays cash on account	Cash Accts. receivable	150	150
	Fixed assets sold for cash	Cash Fixed asset	1,000	1,000
	A sale is made for cash	Cash Cash sales	1,500	1,500
Cash is relocated:				
Deposit	Cash is deposited Bank	X Bank cash Cash	9,750	9,750
	Cash is transferred from X Bank to Y Bank	Y Bank cash X Bank cash	5,000	5,000
Cash is disbursed:				
Adjustment	X Bank service charges are recorded	Bank charges X Bank	5	5
Petty Cash	Postage stamps are purchased	Miscellaneous expense Cash	50	50
Checks	Merchandise is purchased with a check from X Bank	Inventory Bank cash	900	900
	A payment is made to long-term creditors from X Bank	Long-term liability X Bank cash	500	500
	Owner takes draw from Y Bank	Owners draw (Equity) Y Bank cash	1,000	1,000
	Payment is made to vendor from Y Bank	Accounts payable Y Bank cash	250	250
	A fixed asset is purchased with a check/Y Bank	Fixed asset Y Bank cash	2,500	2,500
	Wages, rent, and expenses/Y Bank	Expenses Y Bank cash	400	400
Total			30,505	30,505

Figure 5.2   Cash actions and journal entries.

3. From miscellaneous repetitive sources—for example, rent income, interest income, dividends, and royalties.

4. From miscellaneous repetitive sources—for example, sale of surplus assets or investments and new sources of finance (bank borrowings, loans, equity investment from outside).

Payments

1. To suppliers of raw materials or other suppliers—for example, reduction of accounts payable or notes payable.
2. To employees for salaries and labor related expenses—for example, taxes, insurance, pension, and so on.
3. Utilities and other services where payment is made on a regular basis (telephone, accounting, maintenance, etc.).
4. Other operating expenses (supplies, small tools, fees, etc.).
5. Settlement of tax liabilities (federal, state, and local).
6. For capital expenditures—for example, the acquisition of land, buildings, plant and equipment: representing significant but irregular payments.
7. To meet financial obligations:
   a. Of a regular nature—for example, interest and dividend payments.
   b. Of an irregular nature—for example, repayment of loans.
8. For any other purpose of a significant, irregular or extraordinary nature—for example, settlement of litigation.

Cash Flow in the Small Manufacturing Enterprise.   The Small Business Administration has prepared Management Aid No. 229 for small manufacturers entitled "Cash Flow in a Small Plant."

We have reprinted the management aid here.

INTRODUCTION

"Business is booming. This month alone, the sales volume has risen over 50 percent."

Many proud owner-managers equate growth in sales volume with the success of their enterprise. But, many of these so-called "successful" businesses are becoming insolvent because they do not have enough cash to meet the needs of an increasing sales volume. For, without cash, how can the business pay its bills, meet its payroll requirements, and purchase merchandise for the increased sales demand?

A business must have enough cash to meet its legal obligations and avoid becoming insolvent. This is a primary business objective that may override other objectives, such as sales volume. What good is additional sales volume if you're out of business?

Sufficient cash is one of the keys to maintaining a successful business. Thus, you must understand how cash moves or flows through the business and how planning can remove some of the uncertainties about future requirements.

CASH FLOW

Cash Cycle. In any business there is a continual cycle of events which may increase or decrease the cash balance. The following diagram is used to illustrate this flow of cash.

Cash is decreased in the acquisition of materials and services to produce the finished goods. It is reduced in paying off the amounts owed to suppliers: that is, accounts payable. Then, inventory is sold and these sales generate cash and/or accounts receivable: that is, money owed

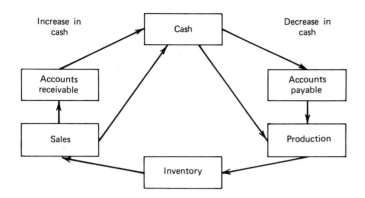

from customers. When customers pay, accounts receivable is reduced and the cash account increases. However, the cash flows are not necessarily related to the sales in that period because customers may pay in the next period.

Net Working Capital. Current assets are those resources of cash and those assets which can be converted to cash within one year or a normal business cycle. These include cash, marketable securities, accounts receivable, inventories, etc. Current liabilities are obligations which become due within one year or a normal business cycle. These include accounts payable, notes payable, accrued expenses payable, etc. You may want to consider current assets as the source of funds which reduce current liabilities.

One way to measure the flow of cash and the firm's ability to maintain its cash or liquid assets is to compute *working capital*. It is the difference between current assets and current liabilities. The change in this value from period to period is called net *working capital*. For example,

	19 × 1	19 × 2
Current assets	$110,000	$200,000
Less current liabilities	−70,000	−112,000
Working capital	40,000	88,000
Net working capital increase (decrease)		$48,000

Net working capital increased during the year, but we don't know how. It could have been all in cash or all in inventory. Or, it may have resulted from a reduction in accounts payable.

Cash Flow Statement. While net working capital shows only the changes in the current position, a "flow" statement can be developed to explain the changes that have occurred in any account during any time period. The cash flow statement is an analysis of the cash inflows and outflows.

The ability to forecast cash requirements is indeed a means of becoming a more efficient manager. If you can determine the cash requirements for any period, you can establish a bank loan in advance, or you can reduce other current asset accounts so that the cash will be made available. Also, when you have excess cash, you can put this cash into productive use to earn a return.

The change in the cash account can be readily determined if you know net working capital and the changes in current liabilities and current assets other than cash.

Let   NWX   be net working capital
          CA   be the change in current assets other than cash
          CL   be the change in current liabilities
      cash   be the change in cash

Since net working capital is the difference between the change in current assets and current liabilities,

$$\text{NWC} = \text{CA (other than cash)} + \text{cash} - \text{CL}$$
$$\text{cash} = \text{NWC} - \text{CA (other than cash)} + \text{CL}$$

This relationship states that if we know net working capital *(NWC)*, the change in current liabilities *(CL)*, and the change in current assets less cash *(CA less cash)*, we can calculate the change in cash. The change in cash is then added to the beginning balance of cash to determine the ending balance.

Suppose you forecast that sales will increase $50,000 and the following will correspondingly change:

Receivables	increase by $25,000
Inventory	increase by $70,000
Accounts payable	increase by $30,000
Notes payable	increase by $10,000

Using net working capital of $48,000, what is the projected change in cash?

$$\text{cash} = \text{NWC} - \text{CA (other than cash)} + \text{CL}$$
$$= 48,000 - 25,000 - 70,000 + 30,000 + 10,000$$
$$= -7,000$$

Conclusion: over this time period, under the condition of increasing sales volume, cash decreases by $7,000. Is there enough cash to cover this decrease? This will depend upon the beginning cash balance.

Sources and Application of Funds. At any given level of sales, it is easier to forecast the required inventory, accounts payable, receivables, etc., than net working capital. To forecast this net working capital account, you must trace the sources and application of funds. Sources of funds increase working capital. Applications of funds decrease working capital. The difference between the sources and applications of funds is the net working capital.

The following calculation is based on the fact that the balance sheet is indeed in "balance." That is, total assets equal total liabilities plus stockholders' equity.

$$\frac{\text{current}}{\text{assets}} + \frac{\text{noncurrent}}{\text{assets}} = \frac{\text{current}}{\text{liabilities}} + \frac{\text{long-term}}{\text{liabilities}} + \text{equity}$$

Rearranging this equation:

$$\frac{\text{current}}{\text{assets}} - \frac{\text{current}}{\text{liabilities}} = \frac{\text{long-term}}{\text{liabilities}} + \text{equity} - \frac{\text{noncurrent}}{\text{assets}}$$

Since the left-hand side of the equation is working capital, the right-hand side must also equal working capital. A change to either side is the net working capital. If long-term liabilities and equity increase or noncurrent assets decrease, net working capital increases. This change would be a source of funds. If noncurrent assets increase or long-term liabilities and equity decrease, net working capital decreases. This change would be an application of funds.

Typical sources of funds or net working capital are

- Funds provided by operations
- Disposal of fixed assets
- Issuance of stock
- Borrowing from a long-term source

To obtain the item, "funds provided by operations," subtract all expense items requiring funds from all revenue that was a source of funds. You can also obtain this result in an easier manner: add back expenses which did not result in inflows or outflows of funds to reported net income.

The most common nonfund expense is depreciation, the allocation of the cost of an asset as an expense over the life of the asset against the future revenues produced. Adjusting net income with depreciation is much simpler than computing revenues and expenses which require funds. Again, depreciation is not a source of funds.

The typical applications of funds or net working capital are

- Purchase of fixed assets
- Payment of dividends
- Retirement of long-term liabilities
- Repurchase of equity

The following is an example of how sources and applications of funds may be used to determine net working capital.

Statement of Sources and Applications of Funds

Sources of funds:		
From operation		
Net income	$ 10,000	
Add depreciation	15,000	
	25,000	
Issuance of debt	175,000	
Issuance of stock	3,000	
	$203,000	
Applications of funds:		
Purchase of plant	$140,000	
Cash dividends	15,000	
	155,000	
Net working capital increase (decrease)		$48,000

Statement of Changes in Financial Position. This statement combines two statements previously discussed: the statement of sources and application of funds and the changes in working capital accounts. This statement can be converted into a cash flow statement by solving for cash as the unknown, as shown below.

Cash Flow Statement

Sources of funds	$203,000	
Applications of funds	155,000	
Net working capital		$ 48,000
Less:		
Increase in receivables	25,000	
Increase in inventory	70,000	−95,000
Plus:		
Increase in accounts payable	30,000	
Increase in notes payable	10,000	40,000
Cash flow		$ −7,000

PLANNING FOR CASH FLOW

Cash flow can be used not only to determine how cash flowed through the business but also as an aid to determine the excess or shortage of cash. Suppose your analysis of cash flow forecasts a potential cash deficiency. You may then do a number of things, such as:

- Increase borrowings: loans, stock issuance, etc.
- Reduce current asset accounts: reduce receivables, inventory, etc.
- Reduce noncurrent assets: postpone expanding the facility, sell off some fixed assets, etc.

By using a cash flow statement you can determine if sufficient funds are available from financing activities, show funds generated from all sources, and show how these funds were applied. Using and adjusting the information gained from this cash flow analysis will help you to know in advance if there will be enough cash to pay

- Bills to suppliers
- Bank loans
- Interest
- Dividends

Careful planning will insure a sufficient amount of cash to meet future obligations on schedule which is essential for the "successful" business.

PLANNING AID

The following example is presented to help you develop a cash flow analysis. Of course, all names are disguised.

During the next month, Irene Smith, owner-manager of Imagine Manufacturing, expects sales to increase to $10,000. Based on past experience, she made this forecast:

Net income to be 9% of sales	$ 900
Income taxes to be 3.2% of sales	320
Accounts receivable to increase	5000
Inventory to increase	2000
Accounts payable to increase	3000

Her beginning cash balance is $3,000 and she plans to purchase a piece of equipment for $1,500. What is her cash flow?

Cash Flow Analysis

Sources of funds:	
Net income	$ 900
Depreciation	1000
	1900
Application of funds	
Addition to fixed assets	$ 1500
Payment of taxes	320
	1820
Net working capital increase (decrease)	80
Working capital accounts	
Less change in	
inventory	$ −2000
accounts receivable	−5000
Plus change in	
Accounts payable	3000
Cash flow	−3920
Plus beginning cash balance	3000
Equals ending cash balance	−920

Assuming Irene's forecast is correct, she has a cash need of $920 next month. If she cannot borrow the additional funds, she must either reduce sales, which may reduce profits, or find another source of cash. She can now use her cash flow analysis to try to determine a source of funds or a reduction in the application of funds. An easy solution is to postpone the purchase of the equipment. This would increase her cash flow by $1,500, more than enough for a positive cash balance at the end of next month.

Forecasting Cash Movements.   Because cash flow is critical to a small manufacturing enterprise, it is essential that management attempt to forecast the likely pattern of future cash flow. Such a forecast will not always be precisely accurate. Nevertheless, it will still create reliable signals to indicate whether, when and what type of action needs to be taken. A "good" forecast is not necessarily the one that turns out to be "right," but the one which, as the future unfolds, provides the basis for guiding appropriate and timely management action.

Here are some of the advantages to a firm which maintains a systematic approach to cash forecasting:

- Costly mistakes can be avoided. Short of bankruptcy, many firms suffer the financial consequences from ill considered or hastily undertaken ventures. A cash forecast will reveal in advance the potential impact on cash flow of any venture. By revealing the possible consequences in advance, there should still be time to reconsider the venture or its timing: it is too late to be wise *after* the event.

- Management control can be facilitated. The cash forecast will provide early warning of an impending cash problem and indicate steps that management might take to reduce or eliminate its impact.

- Confidence of the lender can be increased. It becomes less difficult to raise funds when required if management can demonstrate that it is attempting to be in command of the situation by predicting if, when, for how long, and in what amounts additional funds will be required. It could be too late to attempt to raise funds *after* the onset of financial difficulties.

- Utilization of capital can be improved. Not only is it the function of a cash forecast to indicate cash deficiencies or requirements for finance; it will also indicate if cash surpluses are likely to arise. In these circumstances, management can take appropriate measures to utilize the cash surplus to maximum advantage.

There are two types of cash forecasts: *short-term* and *long-term.* The two types have slightly different objectives and orientation and therefore will be dealt with separately.

The Short-Term Cash Forecast.   The short-term (or short-range) cash budget covers the length of a cycle from investment of cash to its recovery in such terms as inventory and receivables. The period covered is generally one year.

The prime objective of a short-term cash forecast is to ensure that a firm can pay its debts in the immediate future. It is oriented towards the guidance of appropriate management control action in the short term. For this reason, it needs to be up to date and reasonably detailed. It should be prepared at frequent intervals over the next six to 12 months.

Long-Term Cash Forecast.   A long-term (or long-range) cash forecast covers the length of a cycle from investment of cash to its recovery from such items as plant and equipment, market development, and research. The period most commonly used for this purpose is from three to five years, because this is viewed as being the maximum length of time in which sales trends, technology, and the products of market development and research can be projected with sufficient certainty to yield a reliable cash forecast. In cases where long-term cash flow is certain, as with ground rents, mortgage loans or long-term leases, cash flow may be projected accurately for longer periods.

The object of preparing a cash forecast over the longer term is to indicate the financial consequences of future strategic courses of action and to assist in long-term financial planning. This objective is quite different from that of short-term forecasts. The long-term forecast is usually prepared annually. Its orientation is toward the financial consequences of and interrelationships between strategic management decisions.

Cash Control.   There are generally considered to be two types of control in the cash system: 1) stewardship controls, and 2) management controls.

Stewardship Controls.   Stewardship controls are designed to accomplish two things: (1.) the proper receipt of all cash to the organization, and (2.) the proper disbursement of all cash by the organization.

Cash is more susceptible to theft than any other asset, and a large percentage of business transactions involve the receipt and disbursement of cash. For these reasons, strict stewardship controls are needed to prevent misappropriation of cash. Two forms of embezzlement should be noted:

- *Lapping.*   The theft of cash received from one customer, but credited to that customer's account at a later date by using cash received from another customer.
- *Kiting.*   Cashing an unrecorded check in one bank and covering it with a check drawn on another bank. Kiting may also take the form of opening a bank account with a fraudulent check (usually originating in a different city or state to lengthen clearing time), and then drawing most of the amount out before the bank discovers the error.

Embezzlement using the methods described above, or using other techniques, may be guarded against by maintaining a system of internal controls over the handling of cash.

Some general principles for controlling *cash receipts* are:

1. The immediate separation of cash from its documentation. For instance, people who record cash transactions should not write checks or make deposits. Documentation is channeled to the accounting department and cash to the cashier. Their records can be compared.
2. The function of cash handling must be distinct from maintaining the accounting records. Neither party should have access to or supervise the recordkeeping of the other.
3. If possible, there should be a daily deposit of all cash receipts into the bank.
4. The person responsible for cash receipts should not be responsible for cash disbursements.

The following are general principles for controlling *cash* disbursements:

1. All disbursements should be made by check. Issuing a check should require approval of more than one person. A cancelled check is proof that payment was made and payment by check provides a permanent record of disbursements.
2. Checks should be pre-numbered. Spoiled checks should be marked "void."
3. If possible, checks should be signed by one person and countersigned by another.
4. Supporting invoices and other documentation should be perforated or marked "paid" in order to prevent double payment for the same item.

5. A system for approving payments should underlie the issuance of checks. The person who approved payment should not be the person who issues the check.

Note that stewardship controls place a repeated emphasis on the principle of *separation of duties*. Underlying this principle is the fact that the probability of embezzlement is decreased significantly where an act of dishonesty requires the collusion of two or more persons.

Management Controls. The principal purpose of management controls is to *optimize* the company's cash position. This is true if the company has a cash surplus or a cash deficit.

Excess cash may denote poor management, as these cash resources can usually produce a higher return if they are converted to some other form of asset (such as investments). Contrary to popular thinking, a large cash balance is not a reliable indicator of an organization's good state of health; it may be just the opposite. Too little cash is also hazardous: it may require unscheduled borrowing of funds on adverse terms, or the untimely disposition of the firm's assets.

How does one optimize cash position? The application of management controls in administering cash has had some impressive results.

Cash forecasts and budgets are the principal techniques for the management control of cash. Cash budgets may be prepared for any period of time. They serve as management controls for the following reasons:

1. They emphasize the timing of future cash events.
2. They indicate periods when cash surpluses or shortages are likely to occur, thus enabling management to:
   a. Convert temporary surplus cash into investments.
   b. Arrange in advance for financing for periods where shortages are indicated.
3. They facilitate the scheduling of loan repayments.
4. By distinguishing postponable from nonpostponable disbursements, they provide management with a basis for deciding priorities and for relating postponable needs to periods where optimum financing is possible.
5. They provide guidelines for controlling disbursements, in that expenditures for a particular account cannot exceed budget without special approval.

Financial cash flow ratios are another technique for optimizing management controls of cash.

One ratio for doing this is the "average daily disbursements ratio." This is a simple ratio that tells you how much your company spends each day on the average. The formula can be represented as follows:

$$D_a = \frac{D_t}{N_p}$$

Where: D_a = average daily disbursements

D_t = total disbursements for a period

N_p = number of days in the period

Once you know the average amount of money the firm spends daily (the average daily disbursements above), then it is easy to find out how long your cash reserve will last if there is no income. You multiply the average daily disbursements by the number of days to be covered by the cash reserve, as follows:

$$C_b = N_r \times D_a$$

Where: C_b = cash balance

N_r = number of days covered by the cash reserve

D_a = average daily disbursements (from the previous formula)

If you want to find out how many days the cash reserve will last, just turn the formula around like this:

$$N_r = \frac{C_b}{D_b}$$

Example. Hero Manufacturing wishes to maintain a cash balance equal to 20 days of average daily disbursements. Total disbursements for the year is scheduled to be $360,000. The calculations will be based on a standard financial year of 360 days.

$$\textbf{Step 1} \quad D_a = \frac{\$360,000}{360}$$
$$D_a = \$1000$$
$$\textbf{Step 2} \quad C_b = 20 \times \$1000$$
$$C_b = \$20,000$$

There are other ratios that assist management in controlling cash flow, in particular, break-even and cash break-even formulas and accounts receivable and inventory ratios. These ratios will be discussed later.

RECEIVABLES

Generally speaking, the term "receivables" indicates claims for money and goods due from other businesses. There are various types or categories of receivables, including:

- Accounts receivable (due from customers).
- Notes receivabele (due from those who owe money and who have signed a negotiable instrument or note).
- Deposits receivable or returnable.
- Claims against various parties (governments, lawsuits).
- Advances to employees, officers, stockholders.

Current Versus Noncurrent. Receivables may be listed as current assets or as long-term assets. To be classified as a current asset, a receivable should be convertible into cash within one year's time, otherwise it should be classified as a noncurrent asset.

Receivables should be stated at their net realizable cash value. Initially, receivables may be stated at the invoice price of the sale if, for example, a credit sale for $100 is recorded. However, not all receivables are collectible; therefore, to state receivables at their net realizable cash value requires an estimate of the amounts of receivables that will not be collected. In other words, an allowance for bad debts or uncollectible accounts should be deducted from receivables.

Discounting.   It is commonly understood that a dollar today is worth more than a dollar tomorrow. This is because a dollar today can be invested or loaned, and thus interest can be earned.

For example, if you have $100 you can lend this money at 6%. At the end of a year you will have $106, assuming you can collect your principal plus interest from the person you loaned the money to. On the other hand, if a customer buys some goods from you worth $100, but says that he will pay in one year's time, you haven't sold for $100. You only sold for $94 (100 × .94), assuming you could have loaned the money at 6% interest.

A ruling by the Accounting Principles Board (APB),* APB Opinion No. 21,‡ requires that interest by imputed on receivables. This means that if you sell to a customer and allow liberal or lengthy terms for payment without interest on the amounts owed, or interest at an unrealistically low amount, then the amount of the sale and the amount of the receivable should both be reduced by a realistic level of interest on the amounts receivable. This interest is taken into income over the term of the receivable.

Example.   You sell a machine to a customer for $1000 with the following terms: $100 down, balance payable in three annual installments of $300 each, plus accrued interest at 4%.

Amount of sale is $968:	$ 100	down payment
	900	receivable
	72	interest at 4%[3]
	$1072	
	−104	less interest at 6%[4]
	$ 968	

At the end of the first year you would record cash received of $336 and interest income of $52. The difference between the amount of interest income recorded ($52) and the cash interest received ($36) would increase the carrying amount of the receivable from $568 ($868 − $300) to $584.

It should be noted that reducing sales and receivables for imputed interest is required for companies which issue financial statements that conform to generally accepted accounting principles. This is not a procedure that is acceptable for tax purposes, except in certain limited circumstances.

Bad Debts Expense.   When you sell on credit, you must expect some customers not to pay, unless you have an extraordinarily effective collection procedure.

There are four principal methods of calculating estimates of bad debt expense:

• Percentage of sales
• Percentage of credit sales

---

*The APB was the official rule-making body of the accounting between 1959 and 1973. It has been replaced by the Financial Accounting Standards Board.

‡Issued in 1971.

[3](900 × .04) + (600 × .04) + (300 × .04)

[4](900 × .06) + (600 × .06) + (300 × .06)
Amount of receivable composed of: $868

Amount of sale	$968
Less: Cash down	100
	$868

Year	Credit Sales	Actual Bad Debts
1983	$1,000,000	$15,000
1982	900,000	12,000
1981	800,000	12,000
TOTAL	$2,700,000	$39,000

Percentage: $\dfrac{39,000}{2,700,000} = 1.44\%$

1984 Credit sales: $1,200,000
1984 Estimated bad debt expense: 1.44% × $1,200,000 = $17,280

Figure 5.3 Percentage of credit sales method of estimating bad debt expense.

- Percentage of outstanding receivables
- Aging receivables

All of these methods are currently in use. The percentage of credit sales and percentage of outstanding receivables are most commonly used. The aging method probably gives the most accurate figure for bad debts expense and with increased use of computers should become widely used.

Percentage of Credit Sales. When a percentage of sales approach is employed, a company's past experience with uncollectible accounts is analyzed. If there is a stable relationship between previous year's charge sales and bad debts, that relationship can be turned into a percentage and used to determine the current year's bad debt expense (see Figure 5.3).

Percentage of Outstanding Receivables. Using past experience, a company can estimate the percentage of its outstanding accounts receivables that will become uncollectible, without identifying specific accounts. This procedure provides a reasonably accurate picture of the realizable value of the receivables at any time, but does not fit the concept of matching costs and revenues as well as the percentage of sales approach, because you must rely on the past to predict the future (see Figure 5.4).

Year	Accounts Receivable (End of Year)	Accounts Receivable That Become Bad Debts
1983	$150,000	$15,000
1982	140,000	12,000
1981	135,000	12,000
TOTAL	$425,000	$39,000

Percentage: $\dfrac{\$\,39,000}{\$425,000} = 9.2\%$

1984 Ending accounts receivable: $160,000
1984 Estimated bad debt expense: 9.2% × $160,000 = $14,720

Figure 5.4 Percentage of accounts receivable method of estimating bad debt expense.

AGING SCHEDULE

Name of Customer	Balance 12/31	Under 60 Days	61–90 Days	91–120 Days	Over 120 Days
Customer A	$1000	$ 800	$200		
Customer B	3000	3000			
Customer C	600				$600
Customer D	750	600		$150	
	$5350	$4400	$200	$150	$600

SUMMARY

Age	Amount	Percentage	Percentage Amount
Under 60 days	$4400	1%	$444.00
61–90 days	200	5%	10.00
91–120 days	150	10%	15.00
Over 120 days	600	20%	120.00
Bad debts expense			$189.00
Or allowance for doubtful accounts			

Figure 5.5

Aging of Accounts Receivable. A more sophisticated approach than the percentage of outstanding receivables method, is to set up an aging schedule. Such a schedule indicates which accounts require special attention by providing the age of the receivable (see Figure 5.4).

The amount $189.00 indicates the bad debt expense to be reported for the year, but only if this is the first year the company has been in operation. In subsequent years, the allowance for doubtful accounts balance is adjusted to the amount determined by the aging schedule (see Figure 5.5). An aging schedule is not only prepared to determine bad debts expense but it may also serve as a control device to determine the composition of receivables and to identify delinquent accounts. The estimated loss percentage developed for each age category is based on previous loss experience and the advice of persons in your business who are responsible for granting credit. The aging approach is sensitive to the actual status of receivables, but as with all estimates, it may overstate or understate the actual loss from uncollectable accounts.

Designing a Credit Policy. Receivables result from selling on credit, and the essence of credit sales lies in the trade-off between increased sales and increased collection costs. Credit sales can be increased indefinitely in most businesses simply by liberalizing credit agreements. However, the increased sales become unprofitable when the costs of collection exceed the profit margin. Therefore, a balance between increased sales and collection costs must be sought.

Credit rating services, such as Dun and Bradstreet, are useful sources of data for making credit decisions, but rating services cannot make credit granting decisions. They only provide the historical background on a prospective customer.

In making a credit decision, an assessment of a customer's financial position and short-term liquidity is necessary. The most commonly used financial ratio for assessing short-term credit risk is the ratio of current assets to current liabilities.

Based on recent research in the area of prediction of bankruptcy, a better ratio is cash flow to total debt.

Cash Flow to Debt Ratio.   (Cash Flow is approximated by adding depreciation expense to net income and subtracting purchases of fixed assets and dividends.) The ratio of cash flow to total debt will vary by industry, but a ratio of 1:4 may be an expected average. (For public companies, the data is easily obtainable. For privately owned firms, the data will be sought by other means, principally by request of the potential customer.)

Receivables Information System.   In general, a credit policy should be based on the typical credit terms in your industry, and businesses should expect to meet the terms provided by others in the industry. Customers that are poor credit risks require stricter terms. A way to formulate a sound credit policy is to develop a credit information system, sometimes called a credit scoring system. This is based on the five C's of credit: character, capacity, capital, collateral, and conditions.

- *Character.* Defined as the probability that a customer will try to honor his obligations, and measured by past payment history. Interviews and references can supply relevant information.
- *Capital.*   Measured by the financial position of the firm as indicated by total assets, net worth, or debt to equity ratio.
- *Collateral.*   Represented by assets the customer may offer as security.
- *Capacity.*   Measured by the consistency of profitable operations.
- *Conditions.*   The state of the economy and the state of the industry in which the customer operates.

Payment Stimulation Techniques.   The essence of control over receivables is to minimize the amounts of money tied up in receivables while maximizing sales in your particular market. Minimizing the investment in receivables may be facilitated by payment stimulation techniques. Ways to speed up the payment of receivables include:

- Discounts for early payment.
- Add on interest for payment after a certain date.
- Dunning letters that become increasingly threatening as time passes.
- Personal telephone calls.
- Outside collection services.
- Legal action.

Clearly, you would like to stimulate payment with the method that costs least in terms of expense and customer alienation. There is a trade-off between the severity of the stimulation technique and maintenance of customer satisfaction. You should relate the severity of the technique to the age of the receivable.

Accounts Receivable Financing and Factoring.   If you are in a business that is growing rapidly, you may find that there is a need for additional working capital, but that your balance sheet does not support unsecured borrowing from a bank. It is often possible to borrow on a secured basis by pledging or assigning valid accounts receivable as collateral for the loan. Often this type of loan is available from your bank, or from a subsidiary of the bank which specializes in commercial financing. For businesses with higher degrees of risk, commercial finance companies or factors may be the appropriate source of funds.

The type of financing and the terms of the loan will vary by the character of the industry you are in and by the institution providing the financing. However, there are two basic categories of this type of financing: receivables financing and factoring.

Receivable Financing. In receivables financing, receivables act as collateral for a loan. Many types of industries use loans of this type. Typically, the company is growing fast or is highly seasonal and needs cash in order to operate. Financial institutions will take considerable care in validating the value of receivables as collateral. The cost of receivables financing is high compared to the cost of term loans. Whereas the rate on term loans is typically about prime plus one, the rate on receivables loans may be prime plus four or five.

However, there are considerations that make receivables loans attractive. Interest is computed on an average daily basis with receivables loans, while with term loans, interest is computed based on the term. No compensating balances are required with receivables loans. Interest on the nonusable compensating balance at a rate of prime plus one may exceed the additional interest required on a receivables loan.

Factoring. Factoring is distinguished from receivables financing by the fact that in factoring the outstanding receivables are typically sold outright, and without recourse, to the factor. The primary type of factoring is called maturity factoring.

In maturity factoring no funds are remitted by the factor until the receivables are collected. The factor, in essence, serves as the credit department of his customer. Typically the factor knows the customers of the client better than the client knows them, and is able to determine the credit worthiness of a customer and the collectibility of the receivable. The factor maintains credit files on customers in industries where factoring is common, and has staffs of auditors and loan officers to assist collection procedures. For the services, the client pays approximately 1% of outstanding receivables as a factoring fee, but is relieved of collection and credit burdens. Factoring is not widespread outside of the textile and garment industries.

Improvement of Financial Ratios by Factoring. Balance sheet financial ratios may be made to appear more favorable through factoring (see Figure 5.6 which presents an example of comparative balance sheets, with and without factoring). Without factoring, the company requires a $100,000 bank loan and incurs $200,000 of payables, while having $300,000 receivables outstanding. The current ratio is 1.53:1

Without Factoring				With Factoring			
Assets		Liabilities		Assets		Liabilities	
Cash	$ 10,000	Accounts payable	$200,000	Cash	$ 10,000	Accounts payable	$100,000
				Due from factor	100,000	Net worth	160,000
Accounts receivable	300,000	Note payable	100,000	Inventory	150,000		
Inventory	150,000	Net worth	160,000				
Total	$460,000	Total	$460,000	Total	$260,000		$260,000

Figure 5.6 Comparative balance sheets with and without factoring.

without factoring. With factoring, the receivables are sold, and $200,000 is applied to reduce the accounts payable to $100,000 and pay off the note. The current ratio is increased to 2.6:1.

Inventories

The description and measurement of inventories requires careful attention because inventories are one of the most important assets an enterprise possesses. The sale of inventory at a price greater than cost is the primary source of income to most businesses. Matching inventory cost against revenue is necessary for the determination of net income. Inventories are particularly significant because they affect both the balance sheet and the income statement.

Definition of Inventories.   Inventories are defined as assets which are held for sale in the ordinary course of business, or goods that will be used or consumed in the production of goods to be sold. Assets awaiting resale may be excluded from inventory because they are not normally sold in the ordinary course of business.

A manufacturing firm normally has three inventory accounts—raw materials, work in process, and finished goods.

The cost of goods and materials not yet placed into production is considered raw materials inventory. Raw materials are items such as plastic to make toys or steel to make a car. These materials can be traced directly to the end product. At any given point in time in a continuous production process, some units are not completely processed. The cost of the raw material for a partially completed product, plus the cost of labor applied specifically to the material and a share of the overhead costs, constitute the work in process inventory. The costs of completed but unsold units on hand at the end of the period are reported as finished goods inventory.

An example of the three categories of inventories:

Inventories
_____

Finished goods	$200,000
Work in process	15,000
Raw materials	20,000
Other materials and supplies	30,000

The distinction between *inventories* and *supplies* lies in the fact that inventories typically become products to be sold, or at least part of a product to be sold, and supplies are consumed. Supplies would include lubrication oil for a machine, while inventory would include products manufactured by the machine.

From a managerial perspective, inventories are an important asset. The investment in inventories is usually the largest current asset in a small manufacturing enterprise, and it may often be a significant portion of the firm's total assets. If unsalable items accumulate in inventory, a potential loss exists. If products ordered or desired by the customers are not readily available in the style, quality, and quantity required, sales and customers may be lost. Inefficient purchasing, faulty manufacturing, or inadequate sales efforts result in excessive or unsalable inventories.

Inventories are more sensitive to general business fluctuations than other assets. When sales demand is great, merchandise can be disposed of quickly, and large quantities of inventories may appear to be appropriate. Yet, with a downward trend in the business cycle, lines of merchandise will move slowly, stocks will pile up, and obsolescence becomes a spectre hovering over the manager's shoulder.

One essential of inventory planning and control is an accounting system of accurate records, consisting of the information required by management to make manufacturing, merchandising, and financial decisions. Such an accounting system is often referred to as a perpetual inventory system.

In a perpetual inventory system, information is available at any time on the quantity of each item of material or type of merchandise on hand. There are many varieties of such systems in practice. Basically, they may be divided into two types: detailed inventory records that constitute support for the general ledger inventory account or detailed records that do not tie in with the general ledger and constitute an information system outside the accounting double entry system.

In the first type of perpetual inventory system, purchases of raw materials, or inventory of a certain type, are debited directly to an inventory account. As the inventory is sold or transferred to a work in process account, it is credited from the inventory account. Thus, the balance in the inventory account at any time should equal the dollar value of inventory on hand.

In the second type of perpetual inventory system, the records are similar to the first type. The basic difference is that dollar values are not maintained and debits or credits do not enter into the accounting system.

Computers have greatly facilitated the process of inventory control and planning. Because of the data processing capability of computers, additional information can be kept and maintained in the perpetual inventory system. Some types of information that you might want to maintain are: a description of the inventory item, item number, location, minimum and maximum quantities to be maintained in inventory, vendor, amount on order, amount and cost of items on hand.

Regardless of whether the perpetual inventory system is tied into the accounting system or is a separate information system, it is necessary to take a physical inventory periodically. A physical inventory must be taken at least once a year for all inventories. Manufacturing firms take inventories more often in order to maintain control over inventories which can be stolen easily.

In recent years, some companies have developed inventory controls or methods of determining inventories that are effective in determining inventory quantities. These methods are typically based on statistical sampling. The methods may be sufficiently reliable so as to make an annual physical count of each inventory item unnecessary.

Another possibility is to take physical inventories throughout the year on a rotating basis. Thus, instead of taking one annual physical inventory, there is a continued physical inventory throughout the year so that all inventory items are counted and the detailed records corrected at least once during the year.

FIFO versus LIFO.   There are three primary methods of valuing inventory and costs of goods sold for accounting and for tax purposes: (1) first-in, first-out (FIFO), (2) weighted average, and (3) last-in, first-out (LIFO). Figure 5.7 presents an example of the calculation of the ending inventory values and the cost of goods sold under the three methods.

In a period of rising prices, FIFO produces a cost of goods sold figure that is less than the cost of goods sold produced by LIFO. This is the principal advantage of LIFO. The effect of LIFO is to reduce your reported net income and consequently reduce your tax burden.

In certain situations, the LIFO cost flow will be representative of the physical flow of the goods into and out of the inventory. In most situations, however, LIFO will simply be an accounting and tax convention and will not be useful for control of inventory. An advantage of the LIFO method is that it reflects current disposable income. Essentially though, LIFO has become popular for a practical reason: the income tax benefits. As long as the price level of inventories increases and the inventory quantities do not decrease, an indefinite deferral of income taxes occurs. Even if the price level later decreases, your company will have been given a temporary deferral of its income taxes.

There are some criticisms of LIFO that should be mentioned. First, the inventory valuation of the balance sheet is outdated and irrelevant because the oldest costs remain in the inventory. This causes several problems, in particular regarding the measure of working capital of the company. The difference between identical companies, one using FIFO and one using LIFO with respect to working capital will in general be that the working capital under LIFO will be smaller.

Second, LIFO does not measure "real income" in the economic sense. In order to measure "real income" as opposed to monetary income, the cost of goods sold should not consist of the most recently incurred costs, but rather the costs that will be incurred to replace goods that have been sold.

Third, with LIFO you face the involuntary liquidation problem. This problem occurs if the base layers of old costs are liquidated. There can be bizarre results on

	Units	Unit Cost	Total
Assume:			
Beginning inventory	2	$10	$20
Purchases:			
1	1	11	11
2	1	10	10
3	1	12	12
4	1	13	13
Cost of goods available for sale			$66
Total quantity available for sale	6		
Total sold during period	4		
Ending inventory units	2		
Weighted average			
Cost of goods available for sale	$66		
Total units available for sale	6		
Average cost	$11		
Ending inventory value (2 × $11)	$22		
Cost of goods sold (4 × $11)	$44		

First-in, first-out (FIFO)

Ending Inventory: 1 @ 13 = $13
                  1 @ 12 = 12
                           $25

Cost of goods sold:

Cost of goods available for sale	$66
Less: Value of ending inventory	25
	$41

Last-in, first-out (LIFO)

Ending inventory: 2 @ $10 = $20

Cost of goods sold:

Cost of goods available for sale	$66
Less: Value of ending inventory	20
	$46

Figure 5.7   Example of inventory valuation.

income because old costs can be matched against current revenues. Not only can this lead to an overstatement of reported income for a given period, but the income tax consequences could be highly detrimental.

Fourth, in an attempt to avoid the negative consequences of the third criticism above, management may be induced into making poor judgments with respect to inventory purchases. At year end, unnecessary purchases may be made in order to restore liquidated LIFO inventory base layers.

Many companies use LIFO inventories without keeping track of base and incremental layers of items in inventory. They do this by combining many items of inventory together in one so called "pool." The dollars of inventory in this pool at the initial date are considered to be the base layer of the LIFO ending inventory. The actual physical inventory system is maintained on a FIFO basis. At the end of each year the base and incremental layers of inventory are adjusted by a price level index which is based on the change in prices for the year.

NONCURRENT ASSETS

The primary category of noncurrent assets for most businesses is *property, plant and equipment*, which is also referred to as *fixed assets*. Fixed assets are machines, desks, typewriters, buildings, trucks, and land. Virtually all businesses have fixed assets of some sort.

The interesting thing about fixed assets is that all fixed assets except land are subject to depreciation. That is, the fixed assets wear out from use at some point. Even apartment or office buildings, which seem to appreciate, rather than depreciate, in value wear out at some point. Therefore, the Internal Revenue Code allows a deduction on all fixed assets for depreciation.

Depreciation, Depletion, and Amortization

The remainder of this chapter will be concerned with the topic of depreciation. Depreciation, and the related topics of depletion and amortization, is one of the more important areas of accounting and taxation. As the following words will be used frequently in this chapter, here are their definitions:

Depreciation. In accounting terms, depreciation is defined as the process of allocating against revenues the cost expiration of tangible property. Depreciation also carries the connotation of decline in value due to use or wear and tear.

Depletion. Depletion is defined as the process of allocating against revenue the cost expiration of an asset represented by a natural resource, such as an oil well.

Amortization. Amortization is defined as the process of allocating against revenue the cost expiration of intangibles represented by special rights such as patents or leaseholds.

In order to determine the amount of depreciation, depletion, or amortization to be recorded for a period, or which may be deducted for tax purposes, it is essential to know first (1) the cost of the asset, (2) the estimated economic useful life of the asset, and (3) the estimated salvage or residual value of the asset at the end of its useful life.

Example. If you purchase a machine for $11,000 and it has a five year economic life and an estimated salvage value of $1000, then using a straight-line depreciation method, you could record $2000 depreciation expense per year and deduct this amount against revenues and other income in calcualting taxable income.

$$\frac{\$11,000 - \$1000}{5} = \$2000$$

Determining the Cost of an Asset.   The acquisition cost of an asset is measured by the cash outlay made to acquire the asset. If other than cash is exchanged for the asset, the fair market value of the consideration given at the time of the transaction will be the measure of cost. In the absence of a determinable fair market value for consideration given, the asset is recorded at *its* fair market value.

An asset is generally not considered to be acquired for accounting or tax purposes until it has been placed in the position where it is ready to be used and is suitable for production. Thus, all reasonable and legitimate costs incurred in placing an asset in service are considered to be part of the cost.

Cash Purchase.   If an asset is purchased for cash, any outlay that a prudent buyer would make for an asset, including costs of installation, should be capitalized. The capitalizable costs include the invoice price, plus incidental costs such as insurance during transit, freight, duties, title search, registration fees, and installation costs.

Credit Purchases.   If an asset is acquired on a deferred payment basis, the cash equivalent price of the asset, excluding interest, should be capitalized. Actual or imputed interest on the note payable should be charged to current expense when it is paid or accrued. Even if the purchase contract does not specify interest on the liability, imputed interest should be deducted in determining the cost of the asset.

Example.   To illustrate the purchase of an asset on credit, assume the purchase of a machine under a contract that required equal payments of $3154.70 at the end of each of four years when the prevailing interest rate was 10% per annum. To record the asset as $12,618.80 ($3154.70 × 4) would include interest in the cost of the asset. The actual cost of the asset is the present value of the four payments discounted at 10%.

Present value of payments = *Annual Payment* × *Present value of an annuity*

= $3154.70 × 3.1699
= $10,000

Therefore, the cost of the machine would be $10,000. Likewise, the difference between the $10,000 cost and the total of the installment payments ($12,618.80) represents interest expense which may be deducted as it is paid.

Assets Acquired by Exchange for Stocks or Bonds.   If assets are acquired in exchange for stock, the determination of cost may be difficult to achieve. This is because there may be no readily determinable fair market value for the stock or the assets involved. Also, the assets may have been transferred to the business in exchange for stock. This is often a related party transaction, where the owners of the company are contributing assets to the company. The value or cost of both the acquired assets and the associated stock or notes is difficult to determine. As a consequence, the Internal Revenue Code typically indicates that, where assets are transferred to a corporation or a partnership in exchange for ownership interests the cost basis of the asset will be the same in the hands of the corporation as it was in the hands of the transferror/stockholder.

Assets Acquired in Exchange for Other Assets.   If assets are acquired in exchange for other assets, further problems arise regarding the determination of the cost of the acquired assets. Items of property, plant, and equipment are frequently acquired by trading-in an old asset in full or part payment for another asset. In some cases, an asset is acquired by exchanging another asset plus payment or receipt of cash. Cash paid or received in an exchange transaction is often referred to as "boot."

For tax purposes, the cost basis of an asset acquired through an exchange is equal to the cost of the asset given up, plus any cash boot given.

Example.   If a small manufacturing enterprise acquired a truck three years ago for $9000 that has an estimated life of six years, with no salvage value, a straight-line depreciation method is used. The current *book value*, or *basis*, of the truck would be $4500:

$$\$9000 \div 6 = \$1500$$
$$3 \times \$1500 = \$4500$$

If the company traded in the old truck for a new truck and paid $3000 cash in addition, it would then have a new truck with a book value, or basis, for accounting and tax depreciation purposes of $7500, despite the fact that the new truck might have a list price higher or lower than that amount:

$$
\begin{aligned}
\$4500 \\
+3000 \\
\hline
\$7500
\end{aligned}
$$

Investment Tax Credit.   It is important to determine the cost of an asset not only for depreciation purposes, but for an equally valuable reason from a tax perspective, namely the Investment Tax Credit. The Investment Tax Credit was established by Congress in order to stimulate the purchase of machinery and equipment throughout the economy. It was first created in 1962 and has since been modified several times. An investment credit is allowed against tax liability when certain qualified business property is placed into service. The credit may also apply to progress payments made during the course of building or acquiring qualified property. The credit has no effect on regular depreciation.

Taxpayers can take a 10% credit for investments in qualified business property acquired after January 2, 1975. The maximum amount of credit that can be taken in any one taxable year is $25,000, plus 70% of the tax liability in excess of $25,000. By 1982, the limitation will be $25,000 plus 90 percent of the tax liability. This limitation will not affect most individuals or corporations, but for large corporations, with large investments, there may have to be a deferral of the use of the credit to future tax years. The credit can be deferred up to seven years.

The amount of qualified investment depends on the useful life of the property to which the credit applies. It is determined from the cost of used or new property. This is why the cost of an asset is quite important.

Example, if you trade in a machine with a book value of $4000 and pay $1000 cash in addition for a new machine, the cost of the new machine would be $5000, and you would be allowed an investment credit of $500 (10% of $5000).

However, if the machine you acquire is used, rather than new, then only the excess cost above the book value qualifies for the investment credit. Therefore, in the example above, your investment credit would be reduced to $100

($5000 − $4000 × 10%). The reduction in the investment credit for used property has no effect on depreciation. You can still depreciate $5000 of cost over the life of the machine.

The investment tax credit applies to *depreciable tangible personal property*, which means it applies to property used in your trade or business which has a physical existence and which is *not* inventory, supplies, or real estate.

Examples of qualified property include office equipment, machinery in a factory, computers, and neon signs. Even the cost of producing a motion picture or television film has been considered to be qualified property though it is more intangible than tangible. Some costs that are ordinarily considered to be costs of real property qualify for the investment credit if the real property is used as an integral part of either a manufacturing, production, mining, or utility operation, or constitutes a research facility or a facility for bulk storage of commodities. Examples of real property qualifying for the investment credit include blast furnaces, oil derricks, oil and gas pipelines, broadcasting towers, and railroad tracks.

The credit is allowed for the year that the qualifying property is placed into service. This is the earlier of either the first year that depreciation on the asset can be taken, or the year the asset becomes ready for its intended purpose.

There is a limit on the amount of investment in used property and equipment that will qualify for the investment tax credit. The limit is $100,000 for both corporations and individuals.

No investment credit is allowed for property with a useful life of less than three years. Used property will not be qualified if, after you acquire it, it is used by the person from whom you acquired it. An example of this might be a sale and lease-back arrangement. Property which you have used before or property you repossessed will not qualify. Property that you acquire from a subsidiary, or from a parent company if you are a more than 50% owned subsidiary, would not qualify. If you sell or give personally owned property to a business which you control, the business cannot take a credit.

Useful Life Limitations.   In order to qualify for the full investment credit, the useful life of the asset must be at least seven years. If the useful life is five or six years, then only two thirds of the cost of the asset qualifies for the credit. If the useful life is three or four years, then only one third of the cost qualifies. If the useful life is less than three years, the asset does not qualify for the credit.

Example.   Assume that you purchase a truck, a small computer and a lathe.

Asset	Useful life	Cost	Percentage	Qualified amount
Truck	3	$ 9,000	33⅓%	$ 3,000
Computer	5	12,000	66⅔%	8,000
Lathe	7	15,000	100%	15,000
				$26,000

Investment credit ($26,000 × 10%) = $2600

If the credit is not used in the period when it is earned, it may be carried back to offset taxes paid up to three years previously, and may be carried forward up to seven years. Investment tax credits carried forward from previous years are used to reduce current taxes before credits earned in the current year.

The investment credit may have to be recaptured if the asset is not held at least seven years. Even if the asset is destroyed, recapture of the credit will occur.

Example.   If you bought a machine in 1978 which has a useful life of 10 years and cost $8000, in 1978 you could have taken an $800 credit. However, if the machine is destroyed by fire in 1981, the $800 will be added to your tax liability for 1981.

Depreciation Allowance.   Once you have acquired a depreciable asset and have determined its cost, then the question of depreciation arises.

The Internal Revenue Code recognizes that a depreciation allowance is necessary because property gradually approaches a point when its usefulness is exhausted. Therefore, depreciation is allowed only on property that has a definitely limited useful life.

Intangible property can be depreciated, if its use in a business is of limited duration. Examples of depreciable intangibles include licenses, franchises, patents, and copyrights. Ordinarily, depreciation of intangibles is referred to as amortization.

Depreciation Methods.   The Internal Revenue Code specifies three particular methods of computing depreciation. However, others may be used. The three methods are (1) straight line, (2) declining balance, and (3) sum of the years digits.

You do not need to use the same method for all your depreciable property, but once you choose a method for a particular property you must continue to use that method unless you obtain approval from the Internal Revenue Service to change methods. Obtaining approval to change is not a problem. You simply file Form 3115 during the first 180 days of the year of the change.

Useful Life.   You may enter into an agreement with the IRS as to the useful life, depreciation method, and salvage value of any property. However, there are classes of property that have been established by Internal Revenue regulations. These classes each have asset depreciation ranges. If you choose a useful life within the limits of the asset depreciation range for a given asset, you will not be challenged by the IRS.

Salvage value, established at the point when property is acquired, is the amount that can be realized when the property is no longer useful to the taxpayer. It may be no more than junk value, or it may be a large portion of the original cost, depending on the length of time before the end of the asset's useful economic life. This is determined by when the taxpayer plans to dispose of it. An estimated salvage value of *less than 10%* of original cost may be disregarded in computing depreciation. However, no asset may be depreciated below a reasonable salvage value.

Salvage value must be subtracted from original cost in computing straight line and sum of the years digits depreciation. It is *not* subtracted in computing declining balance depreciation.

Example.   A machine is purchased for $10,000 which has a salvage value of $2000 and a useful life of five years. The first year's depreciation using each of the three methods is as follows:

- *Straight line.* $10,000 minus $2000 divided by five $= $1600
- *Sum of the years digits.* $10,000 minus $2000 times $^5/_{15} = $2667
- *Double declining balance.* $10,000 times 40% $= $4000

Straight Line.   The formula for straight line depreciation is: Cost minus salvage value divided by useful life equals depreciation for each year.

Sum of the Years Digits.   Sum of the years digits depreciation allocates a declining portion of the total cost to depreciation expense in each year. In the example shown above where a machine was purchased for $10,000 and had a salvage value of $2000 and a useful life of five years, sum of the years digits depreciation would be calculated as follows:

Year	Factor	×	Cost minus salvage	=	Depreciation expense
1	5/15		$8000		$2667
2	4/15		8000		2133
3	3/15		8000		1600
4	2/15		8000		1067
5	1/15		8000		533
Total					$8000

A useful formula for calculating the denominator of the sum-of-the-years digits fraction is:

$$\frac{n\ (n\ +\ 1)}{2}$$

Where n = useful life

Example. Useful life $\ \ =$ 10 years
Denominator $= \dfrac{10\ \times\ 11}{2} = 55$

Double Declining Balance. The declining balance method applies a constant percentage to the declining book value of the asset.

Example. The cost of machine is $10,000, and its useful life is five years.

Year	Percentage	Book value	Depreciation
1	40%	$10,000	$4000
2	40%	6,000	2400
3	40%	3,600	1400
4	40%	2,160	864
5	40%	1,296	518.40

Note that the total depreciation exceeds the original cost minus salvage value of $8000. This would *not* be allowed for tax purposes. Therefore, in the fourth year only $160 of depreciation could be taken (in order to bring the book value equal to the salvage value), and in the fifth year no depreciation would be taken.

The maximum rate on declining balance depreciation is specified by the following table. The factor is multiplied by the straight line rate in order to find the maximum declining balance rate.

Type of Property	Factor
New equipment	2
Used equipment	1½
New real estate	1½
Used real estate	1
Used residential rental property	1¼

Usually when you acquire an asset during a year, you prorate the depreciation that you owe on the asset.

Example.   On April 1, you acquire a machine for $12,000 which has a useful life of 10 years. You decide to use straight line depreciation. The depreciation expense for the year of acquisition would be $900 [($12,000/10) $\times \frac{9}{12}$].

Chapter Six
Liabilities

Liabilities are the amounts a company owes. Liabilities are obligations that result from past transactions and require the payment of assets (cash), or rendering of services, in the future. Liabilities are usually definite in amount, or subject to reasonable estimation. The amounts are stated or implied in oral or written contracts.

Liabilities can be classified into current and noncurrent. *Current liabilities* are those which are due and payable within one year. They include such things as salaries and wages payable; other accrued expenses such as utilities, taxes, and supplies; accounts payable for inventories; short-term notes payable to banks and others.

We have previously discussed inventories, and there is not much more to be said about the accounts payable side of inventories. The most important thing to remember is to keep track of accounts payable for inventory in a purchases and cash disbursements journal.

Salaries and wages payable and other accrued expenses are really another side of expenses and cash disbursements. We have previously discussed cash disbursements arising from operating expenses. The main thing to remember with accrued expenses is to keep track of cash disbursements by using a check register and cash disbursements journal.

The other current liabilities typically represent debt due to banks and others, and are usually documented by a note. A note is a form of I.O.U., and is usually a legal document. This means that the holder of the note can take it to a court in order to have its provisions enforced.

Noncurrent liabilities are those which are due and payable in more than one year's time. Noncurrent liabilities are also referred to as *long-term debt*. Nearly all long-term debt is evidenced by a note. So notes pertain to both long-term and short-term debt.

DEBT

Every business in the United States regardless of size must from time to time borrow money. Usually a business will borrow from a bank, but it may also borrow from commercial finance companies; state, local, and federal governments; and the public bond market. The larger the business, the more likely that they can tap all of these debt sources. The smaller the business, the more likely that they will only be able to use banks, government, and commercial loan sources.

Because this chapter of necessity is limited in scope, we shall not discuss publicly issued bonds. This is a specialty operation that requires accountants, lawyers, and underwriters. Moreover, most businesses in the United States will never be in a position to sell public bonds. We will limit the discussion in this chapter to the traditional sources of debt capital: banks, commercial financial lenders, and government (such as Small Business Administration loans).

FINANCIAL LEVERAGE

Financial leverage is defined as the ratio of total debt to total assets. For example, a firm having assets of $1 million and total debt of $500,000 has a leverage factor of 50% ($500,000/$1,000,000).

The best way to understand the proper use of financial leverage is to analyze its impact on profitability under varying conditions. Let's take the example of three firms in the electronic parts industry that are identical except for their debt percentage. Company A has used no debt and consequently has a leverage factor of zero. Company B is financed by half by debt and half by equity so its leverage factor is 50%. Company C has a leverage factor of 75%. The companies' balance sheets are shown in Figure 6.1.

A company's capitalization affects stockholder returns in a manner dependant on the state of the economy and conditions in the industry. For example, let us assume that when the economy is depressed the firms can earn 4% on assets because sales and profit margins are low. When the economy is brighter, the firms can earn 8%. Under normal conditions they will earn 11%, under good conditions 15%, and they can earn a 20% rate of return on assets if the economy is very good. The following table illustrates how the use of financial leverage magnifies the impact on stockholders (or firm owners) and relates directly to changes in the rate of return on assets (see Figure 6.2).

As shown in the illustrations, when economic conditions go from normal to good, return on assets for Company A (no leverage) goes up 36.4%, return on equity for Company B (50% leverage) increase 57.1%, and return on equity for Company C (75% leverage) goes up a full 80%. Just the reverse happens when the economy is depressed. When the economy drops from normal to poor, Company A's return on equity declines only 27%; whereas Company B which has a higher leverage has a decline in return on equity of 42.9%. Company C, which has the highest leverage,

		Company A		
		Total debt	$-0-	
		Net worth	$100	
Total assets	$100	Total liability and worth	$100	
		Company B		
		Total debt	$ 50	
		Net worth	50	
Total assets	$100	Total liability and worth	$100	
		Company C		
		Total debt (8%)	$ 75	
		Net worth	25	
Total assets	$100	Total liability and worth	$100	

Figure 6.1

	Very Poor	Poor	Normal	Good	Very Good
Rate of return on total assets before interest	4%	8%	11%	15%	20%
Dollar return on total assets before interest	$4	$8	$11	$15	$20
Company A (No Leverage)					
Earnings in dollars	$4	8	11	15	20
Less: Interest expense	$0	0	0	0	0
Gross income	$4	8	11	15	20
taxes (50%)*	$2	5	5.5	7.5	10
Available to owners	$2	4	5.5	7.5	10
Percentage return on equity	2%	4%	5.5%	7.5%	10%
Company B (Leverage (50%)					
Earnings in dollars	$4	8	11	15	20
Less: Interest expense	$4	4	4	4	4
Gross income	$0	4	7	11	16
Taxes (50%)*	$0	2	3.5	5.5	8
Available to owners	$0	2	3.5	5.5	8
Percentage return on equity	0%	4%	7%	11%	16%
Company C (Leverage 75%)					
Earnings in dollars	$4	8	11	15	20
Less: Interest expense	$6	6	6	6	6
Gross income	$(2)	2	5	9	14
Taxes (50%)*	$(1)	1	2.5	4.5	7
Available to owners	$(1)	1	2.5	4.5	7
Percentage return on equity	-4%	4%	10%	18%	28%

*The tax calculation assumes tax credits for losses

Figure 6.2. Economic conditions.

shows a decline in return on equity of a full 60%. In other words, the companies with the highest leverage (most debt as a percentage of total assets) receive the best return for owners' capital in normal or good times, but the worst return for owners' equity in depressed economic times. The companies with the least leverage (least debt as a percentage of total assets) reap the highest relative return in times of a depressed economy.

As one would expect, wide variations on the use of financial leverage may be observed among industries and among individual firms in each industry. Financial institutions use the most leverage. Financial institutions typically have high liabilities. Public utility use of debt stems from a heavy fixed asset investment coupled with extremely stable sales. Mining and manufacturing firms use relatively less debt because of their exposure to fluctuating sales. Small firms as a group are heavy users of debt. In the manufacturing industries, wide variations in leverage are observed for individual industries. The lowest debt ratios are found in textile manufacturing because their competitive pressures tend to be great. Low debt ratios are also found in the durable goods industries. The highest reliance on debt is found in consumer nondurable goods industries where demand is relatively insensitive to fluctuations in general business activity.

SOURCES OF DEBT CAPITAL

Excluding public debt offerings, there are basically three sources for debt capital: banks, commercial finance companies, and government agencies.

Banks

The advantages of securing a bank loan are:

1. Generally, with the exception of a few government and private programs, borrowing from a bank is the least expensive way to borrow.
2. Borrowing from a bank, as opposed to a government or commercial source, is usually better for your credit rating.
3. Banks have the largest loan breadth—that is, more types of loans, more sources.
4. Banks offer many business services, including credit references on customers or potential customers; financial, investment, and estate advisory services; discounting services for customers' accounts and notes payable; safe deposit boxes; night depositories.

The disadvantages of dealing with banks include:

1. The financially conservative nature of banks may cause problems; that is, bank loans are the most difficult of the loans to obtain.
2. In banks that have a large number of branches, there is a tendency to have a branch manager work at one branch for only a couple of years. Therefore it is difficult to establish a long-term relationship with a branch manager.
3. The technical requirements (financial statements, projected budgets, corporate and ownership information, etc.) of obtaining a loan are greater with a bank than with other sources.
4. Because banks are regulated by the federal government, and are at the same time profit-making organizations, they have to be careful of their loans. For most long-term loans, banks demand annual, semi-annual, quarterly, or even monthly income statements and balance sheets so that they can observe your business carefully.

What is the best time and the worst time to approach a bank for money? Of course, depending on your personal or company situation, any time might be a good time or bad time, irrespective of external influences and bank policies. That is, you might fall into the category of what we call the unwritten golden rule of borrowing, which says: "If you don't need money, that's the best time to get a loan."

The best environment for borrowing is:

1. When interest rates are generally low. This means two things, that the bank has more money to loan than it usually does and that the borrower will get a better deal.
2. When a bank has just opened. New banks, especially independent banks, are looking for business, especially deposit business. Newly opened banks will take more chances with a marginal business because they have to build up their loan portfolio. Sometimes you will find that new banks are conservative; but if you start building a relationship immediately, and you don't ask for a loan at the start, the bank will loan to you when they get to know you. Incidentally, if you

have a sizable business, banking with a small independent will be good because you might be their biggest depositor. If you are their biggest depositor, they will provide better service.

3. When the economy is in an up-turn; that is, when sales throughout the economy are increasing, the stock market is up, and disposable consumer income is up. This might be reflected in lower interest rates.

4. When banks in a particular area are in heavy competition. This might mean that there are too many banks in a new, developing area. Some ways that you can tell there is a lot of competition is if more than one bank visits your business to start up a relationship. Another sign is when there are a lot of incentives for deposits; that is, when banks try to out do themselves in the premiums they offer for deposits.

5. When banks are in a generally expansionary process. During the 1960s, banks downplayed the traditional conservatism and started expanding their branch systems—including international branches—tremendously. Since there was more competition and a downgrading of traditional restraints, money was easier to obtain. There is a new facet of banking that might spark expansion: electronic banking devices called consumer-bank communication terminals, or CBCTs. These are the electronic devices that banks put outside their banches, or in supermarkets, shopping centers, and so on. These devices provide money or allow you to deposit without ever going to the bank. If the use of these devices becomes widespread, the banks that get the most deposits will have more money to loan.

6. When there is a special program within the bank, usually a large bank, to take high-risk loans as "the bank's moral obligation." An example of this is loans to minorities and special groups such as veterans, the handicapped, and—in some cases—displaced businesses or disaster victims. The large banks sometimes set aside sums for these "special high-risk" loans; but beware, regardless of the bank's good intentions, if the economy is bad or there is a high demand on loan funds, these special loans have a way of being forced out.

The worst environment for borrowing is:

1. When interest rates are high. When rates are high there is a large demand on bank funds, and in many cases, from large, secure "Fortune 500" type firms. Also, at these times, the bank might be able to raise its loan limit. High interest rates mean not only that money is more expensive, but that there is less of it to borrow.

2. When the economy is in a recession. In recessionary times, regardless of other influences, banks tend to be more conservative in their lending. There are more chances for a business to go under in a recession. Furthermore, there is usually high demand for money to tide an established business over.

3. When a bank has reached its lending limit, or when the bank has made a decision to decrease its dollars outstanding to make the bank more liquid. When there is an extremely high demand for funds, the bank is tempted to loan at high rates and therefore make a better profit. There is a limit as to how much money it can loan out, however, and that limit is its maximum loan-to-deposit ratio. The loan-to-deposit ratio is simply the total loans it has outstanding divided by the total number of deposits it has. During 1974, the banks were sometimes up to 75% of their deposits loaned out. This was difficult for the banks because if only 26% of their depositors took out their money, the bank would be in serious trouble—perhaps bankruptcy. Even this 75% loan-to-

deposit ratio might be misleading. Banks have to report their loan-to-deposit ratio to the federal government once a week. They can borrow money from other banks for 24 hours to bring up their deposits to help the ratio. In the early part of the twentieth century the banks would very seldom go above 33% loan-to-deposit ratio.

In 1975, when money supply increased, loans did not. The reason was that although more money was available to loan out, the banks wanted to keep the money to build up their loan-to-deposit ratio.

4. When there is very little bank competition for loans and deposits. A one bank town is a perfect example. When you need money, you go there and the competition is nil. The best thing to do is go to another town for financing.

5. When the bank is in trouble or suffers severe losses. In 1973, when United California Bank had trouble with its Swiss subsidiary, it was very difficult to get financing from the branches.

Of course, it is not always possible to wait for the right time to get a loan, and chances are good you will need money the most when everyone else needs it.

Commercial Lenders

Commercial lenders, including commercial finance companies, life insurance companies, foundations, and other private financial companies, are usually more expensive than banks, but they make more loans to a broader class of customers than banks.

Commercial lenders, in general, are willing to loan to businesses that are not as strong financially as the businesses that banks would consider. Furthermore, commercial lenders are willing to take as collateral items which banks would be more selective about, such as inventories and receivables. In short, the major advantage of commercial lenders is their flexibility.

The major disadvantage of commercial lenders is that their interest rates are generally higher and sometimes much higher than banks.

Life insurance companies, pension funds, and foundations offer money to business for real estate, equipment, and sometimes working capital, in amounts that are usually greater than the typical bank loans. Their interest rates are usually only slightly higher than banks. The disadvantage of these companies is that they usually only make large loans (in excess of $1 million) and require that the applicant companies be financially strong. This generally eliminates most small business from consideration.

Government Loans

The largest single lender to business in the United States is the federal government, followed by state and local governments. The federal government lending program is larger than the loan programs of Bank of America, Chase Manhattan, Citibank, J.P.Morgan, and the rest of the ten largest banks in America. The United States government loans over $1.852 trillion per year to business.

Without question, the cheapest loans available in this country are those made by the government. Unfortunately, only a few special businesses, under very special circumstances, qualify for these loans. Most businesses, however, do qualify for government loans that have interest at a few points above prime. Although most government loans carry interest rates that are the same as or a little higher than bank rates, the government will make loans to businesses with higher risk than the banks.

For instances, a start-up business that requires $100,000 in capital and has only $35,000 would not qualify for a loan at a bank at *any* interest rate. The same business, however, would qualify for a Small Business Administration (SBA) loan at close to bank interest rates.

The equity requirements for most government loans are also less than those of a bank. For a start-up business, banks usually require 50% equity, whereas government loans require from 10% to 45% equity. For instance, let us take the example of a person who wants to start a business and has $15,000 in cash. At the bank he would be eligible for a maximum loan of another $15,000, for a total of $30,000. If the same person applied for a government loan, he could receive $18,300 to $150,000, depending on the loan program. Starting a business with $45,000 instead of $30,000 can make a big difference in the long-range success of that business.

The repayment period for government loans is also usually longer than that for bank loans. For this reason, the monthly payment is usually lower for a government loan. For example, if a business borrows $10,000 for three years at 10.25%, the monthly payments are $323.85. If, on the other hand, the same firm borrows the same amount ($10,000) at the same interest rate (10.25%) for *seven* years instead of three years, the monthly payments are $167.31, or $156.54 less than the 3 year loan.

Along with the advantages to government loans there are some significant disadvantages. Government loans and government guaranteed loans take from two months to two years to receive approval. The effort required in paperwork and research is much gerater than for a bank loan or a commercial loan. In short, the greatest disadvantages of government loans is time required for approval and the paperwork involved.

TYPES OF LOANS AVAILABLE FROM BANKS, COMMERCIAL, AND GOVERNMENT LENDERS

The following is a listing of the types of loans that are available and a brief discussion of the type of financing where each is used.

Bank Loans

Loans for 30 to 90 day periods are called *short term loans*. Short-term loans are usually employed to finance inventory on which the business can expect to get a cash return in a short period of time. New businesses very seldom receive this type of loan because most businesses cannot turn their money around during the first few months of operations. However, short-term loans are used extensively for existing businesses.

Intermediate term loans are for periods of more than one year but less than five years. Equipment loans fall into this category. Most businesses that request bank loans will receive this type of loan unless they are financing property.

Long-term loans are for periods of five years or more. Government guaranteed loans are usually for more than five years. Banks will also make long-term loans on property and property improvements.

Besides being named for the term they are for (term loans), loans are further classified into secured and unsecured loans. *Secured Loans* are loans that require security. That means that the business has to pledge some physical thing of value as security or collateral for the loan. A loan for buying equipment is a secured loan, because equipment is pledged as security. The bank can repossess in the event the borrower is unable to make the payments. *Unsecured loans* have no collateral pledged. Unsecured loans are made on the strength of your credit in general and in particular with that bank.

Only the rare business getting started or attempting extensive expansion will obtain an unsecured loan. Even government guaranteed loans are "partially secured" (not totally supported by collateral, but supported with collateral to a large extent).

Secured loans fall into four categories: loans secured by liquid assets (stocks, bonds, or cash), loans secured by accounts receivable, loans secured by inventory, and loans secured by fixed assets (equipment, improvements, and property).

Liquid asset loans are loans that use savings accounts, stocks, or bonds for collateral. Usually with this kind of loan the business leaves its stock, bonds, or savings with the bank and the bank loans an amount equal to (for savings) or less than (with stocks and bonds whose market value fluctuates) the amount of the security. The advantage of this type of loan is that the interest rate charged is low (1% to 2% above that earned on savings, or near prime in the case of stocks or bonds).

Accounts receivable secured loans which include both factoring and accounts receivables financing are not available to a business just starting out. Accounts receivable financing, and more especially factoring, tend to be expensive ways to finance a business. This type of financing is best used in a situation where sales are growing faster than cash flow. In accounts receivable financing (which has lower interest rate than factoring), the lender loans up to 80% of the value of the receivables (assuming all the accounts are reasonably good). The customer pays the firm and the firm assigns the endorsed check to the lender. In factoring, the lender buys the firm's accounts. When a factor buys receivables, the customer pays the factor directly and receives a statement saying that the account is owned by that factor.

Inventory loans are made to businesses where there is an amount of inventory which will be tied up for a long period of time. One example of this type of business is a car dealership. It is necessary for the dealership to retain expensive inventory (cars) in the showroom for long periods of time before the cars are sold. In case of a car dealership, the company has physical possession of the inventory, but the bank owns the title. The type of inventory financing used for a new car dealership is called "flooring" (the borrower keeps the merchandise on the floor). Inventory loans are not made for inventory which is made up of numerous items of different prices (grocery, hardware, and most retail businesses), fast selling items, or is work-in-process (the uncompleted goods in manufacturing). You can, however, borrow on this nonfinanced inventory if you receive a business loan (rather than an inventory loan) which includes other items like equipment, signs, and additional property.

Fixed asset secured loans are for large "capital" items like equipment, land and buildings, improvements, and fixtures. Fixed asset loans are usually for the longest period of all the secured loans previously discussed. Real estate loans are a good example of secured fixed asset loans. All fixed asset loans are for terms of at least two years and usually exceed five years in length.

Government guaranteed loans are the kind of loans that should interest most small businesses. For the vast majority of small businesses just beginning, the best government guaranteed loan is the Samll Business Administration (SBA) guaranteed loan. The SBA loan guarantees the bank 90% against loss. That means that when you borrow $100,000 from a bank with a SBA guarantee, if you lose all the money in the first week, the bank will be paid 90% of the loss, or $90,000 by the SBA. The SBA guaranteed loan is for high risk types of business—that is, small, and especially new businesses. The borrower has to meet other requirements; information is available from the local SBA office. In most cases, however, small and new "start-up" businesses qualify.

Commercial Finance Companies

Types of loans available from commercial finance companies include inventory loans, equipment and fixture loans (including commercial time financing), accounts receivable loans (including accounts receivable financing), and equipment leasing (leasing companies). The types of loans will be covered in order:

Inventory loans are available to accounts receivable and factoring clients. Such loans are frequently utilized to assist the customer during periods of slow product shipments and inventory build-up, or to facilitate bulk raw material purchases at advantageous prices.

Equipment loans include basically two types: money loaned against presently owned equipment, and money loaned to finance new equipment and financed on a time sales financing basis.

On presently owned equipment, commercial finance companies will sometimes make loans. These advances are normally paid back monthly over a period one to five years. The proceeds from this type of loan may be used by the borrower to increase working capital, reduce accounts payable, or simply to purchase new equipment. Very often an equipment loan is accepted in conjunction with accounts receivable or factoring arrangements.

Industrial time sales financing is the process of a company buying equipment from an equipment supplier and the equipment supplier selling the purchase contract to a financier.

The price you pay for buying equipment on installment is usually high; higher, in fact, than the highest interest allowable in your state.

The cost of buying on installment, called the "time price differential," has the following rationale: A seller is presumed to have two prices. One is the cash price; the other price is the "time price," which assumes that the purchaser, who wants credit over a period of time, must pay an added charge to compensate the seller for his additional burden. The differential between the cash price and the time price is the time price differential. This reasoning assumes that the seller is not a money lender. This theory provides the legal mechanism to remove the time sale from the application of usury laws (the state laws that restrict the maximum interest that can be charged on secured loans) in holding that the transaction is a credit sale and is neither a loan nor a forebearance for money.

Accounts receivable loans are the "bread and butter" of commercial finance companies, and were originally what the commercial finance companies were set up to deal with. Accounts receivable loans fall into two categories: accounts receivable financing and factoring.

Accounts receivable financing at banks is practically identical to accounts receivable financing by commercial finance companies.

Accounts receivable can be pledged as collateral for loans. Typically, an 80% advance is made against eligible accounts. The assignment is handled on a nonnotification, revolving basis and is self-liquidating. Interest charges are billed on the basis of actual daily cash loan balances. This monthly charge is frequently less than missed cash discounts.

Leasing is also a type of financing. It is a way of financing 100% of the purchase price of equipment. Leasing is the infant of the traditional, popular, funding methods, and there is some debate as to whether it is a good method of finance. To add to the controversy, there is no standard way things can be leased. You can rent equipment with or without maintenance, or with partial maintenance, or you can lease by the month, year, or several years. You can also obtain leases with the option to purchase.

Life insurance companies. Because of the growth of the insurance industry, the accumulation of assets in insurance companies has been rapid and substantial. It has been estimated that these companies are accumulating assets at the rate of $6 billion per year. The outflow of their funds to pay claims can be statistically predicted. Hence, a part of their portfolio is available for long-term financing in the form of mortgages on industrial, commercial, and housing real estate. Insurance companies also make loans to businesses, but require substantial enterprises with long earnings records dealing in markets not subject to rapid change. The average small or medium sized business would not qualify because insurance companies must follow certain loan policies: (1) the borrower has to be a corporation, (2) there is a minimum time for the borrower to be in business, (3) the borrower should have sufficient historical and current earnings to meet obligations, including debt repayments. An insurance company grants two types of loans: commercial and industrial mortgage loans and unsecured loans. Mortgages by insurance companies cost the same as more orthodox bank loans.

A prevalent type of life insurance company loan is on an unsecured basis to a business in a very good financial condition. Life insurance lenders are most interested in long-range financial data demonstrated by projected sales, cash flows, and so on.

Other Sources. Besides the sources mentioned, there are other less known sources of capital. These include credit union and pension funds and foundations.

Credit Unions. If you are a member of a credit union, you can receive reasonable interest loans for small amounts. Credit union services are offered only to members of credit unions; the credit union law restricts membership in a single credit union to a more or less homogeneous group of members having a common bond of interest. Credit union laws restrict the rate of interest charged and the amount of loan that may be made to a single borrower.

Pension Funds and Foundations. Because of the growth of pension funds, such funds have experienced a rapid accumulation of assets. Their standards of investment are similar to those of the life insurance companies, and they charge about the same interest rates.

A good percentage of pension fund money is used for sale-lease back arrangements.

Government Loans

Guidelines for government loans differ with each organization that can grant loans, but generally the government tries to aid business to increase employment when it would otherwise be difficult for the business alone to do so. The government guarantees loans to businesses in financial situations that banks and other financial institutions can not or will not approach. Private and commercial lenders may not make the loan if it is too large, too risky, or does not fall into the traditional lending categories.

Government loans are not easy to obtain, but sometimes government agencies loan money to extremely high risk businesses, and the interest rate is usually low. However, the loan requirements are generally quite complicated.

Applying for government loans requires considerable time and effort, not the least of which is the time involved to prepare the necessary documentation. The technical requirements—that is, the proposal (analysis of your business, including budgets)— require much detail and technical work. If a firm decides to apply for government loans it is advisable to consult a specialist in this field. An excellent reference is *Business Loans: A Guide to Money Sources and How to Approach Them Successfully* by one of the authors of this book, Rick Stephen Hayes, published in 1977 by CBI of Boston. This book covers all the procedures and requirements of government loans in detail.

ACCOUNTING IMPLICATION OF DEBT

When a lender loans money to a business, the immediate entry is a credit to a note payable account, with an explanation of the terms and length of the loan, as follows:

GENERAL JOURNAL

Date	Comment	Debit	Credit
4/7/79	Cash	$17,000	
	Notes payable		$17,000
	To record 15%, 120 month note from Bank of Amerigold, payments are $263.95 per month.		

Whenever a payment is made to Bank of Amerigold, a portion of that payment will be interest, and a portion will be principal. Interest is the amount of money that the lender charges for using the loan. Principal is that amount of the loan repayment that is applied toward reducing the balance owed. Interest is an expense and should be posted to an expense account. Principal is a reduction of the debt and is posted directly as a debit (a reduction in the amount owed) to the note payable account.

Each month the lender notifies the borrower how much of the monthly payment is interest ($263.95 in the example) and how much is principal.

Using as our monthly payment $263.95, the interest amount of the loan as 14%, and the amount of the loan as $17,000 (as in the example above), we get the following monthly transactions:

GENERAL JOURNAL

Date	Comment	Debit	Credit
5/20/79	Interest Expense	$198.33	
	Note Payable	65.62	
	Cash		$263.95
	To record monthly payment of note to Bank Amerigold		

The interest expense is tax deductible in the year of entry. Principal payments are not a tax deductible expense, but are a reduction in the balance owed on the loan. After all payments are made (120 in this example), the note is paid off and the liability is reduced to zero.

When the small manufacturing enterprise issues financial statements for banks, stockholders, government agencies, or other interested parties, a footnote should be included with these financial statements indicating the term and interest amount of the loan and the name of the asset secured by the note, if any.

Chapter Seven
Cost Accounting

JOB-ORDER COSTING*

A cost accounting system should provide cost figures that will enable a small manufacturing enterprise to make decisions such as the following for each type of good manufactured:

1. How profitable is the product at present prices?
2. Can it be profitably produced to sell at a different price?
3. At what price should it be sold?
4. Should its production level be expanded (or reduced)?
5. What can be done to control costs?

If only a few kinds of products are made and the manufacturing process are always the same, these decisions can be made on the basis of average cost figures per unit computed each month. Either of two methods can be used to compute the average costs: (1) divide the total manufacturing cost by the number of product units produced or (2) compute the unit costs of the individual processes and total them. In both cases, in figuring the number of units produced, changes in the inventory in process must be taken into consideration.

Suppose, on the other hand, that many different types of products are made and that pricing is based on costs. This is likely to be the case where a job order plant produces goods for different customers to the individual customers' specifications, or for a single customer whose specifications change often, or for the government.

In such cases, the cost accounting system must be set up so that product costs can be determined more directly. These systems are referred to as job order cost systems. If each product unit requires a large dollar outlay, costs are assigned directly to each unit. For less costly units, costs may be assigned to groups or batches of similar items and unit costs computed as an average for each group. Job order costing may also have a departmental basis—for example, Department A—Welding, Department B—Cutting and Assembling, Department C—Maintenance, Department D—Planning and Engineering.

COST ACCOUNTING JOURNALS AND LEDGERS

The cost accounting system for any manufacturing enterprise should include an integrated group of journals, ledgers, basic cost records, and control records. The

*Adapted from "Cost Accounting for Small Manufacturers," Small Business Management Series Number Nine, 2nd Edition, U.S. Small Business Administration.

number and kinds of journals and ledgers will depend on (1) the type and volume of transactions, and (2) the type and volume of cost transfers made necessary by the manufacturing techniques.

For a small manufacturing enterprise, a combined journal from which all postings to general and factory ledger accounts can be made is often satisfactory. If the volume of entries is large enough to require several persons for bookkeeping, separate books of original entry such as the following will be needed:

1. Voucher register
2. Check register
3. Cash receipts journal
4. Sales journal
5. Factory journal
6. Payroll journal

If all activities—manufacturing, administrative, and selling—are carried on in a single location, a general ledger with some subsidiary records is adequate. Subsidiary records will be needed for production jobs and certain other items such as accounts receivable, raw materials, and accounts payable.

If the general office is not at the same location as the factory, it is usually best to use a factory ledger in addition to the general ledger. Reciprocal accounts in each of the ledgers show the net balances of the accounts in the other ledger and so provide for self-balancing. In this way, many of the details of accounting for manufacturing costs can be confined to the factory ledger.

CONTROLS AND COST PROCEDURES FOR A JOB-ORDER PLANT

The distinctive features of a job-order cost system are in the basic cost and control records. A typical set of these records will include the following:

Orders and reports containing physical-product information:
1. Job order
2. Job control record
3. Daily production report
4. Job-order instruction card

Orders and reports containing both physical-product and dollar-cost information:
1. Material requisition
2. Job timecard
3. Job-cost record
4. Production-cost summary

Control Records

The orders and reports containing physical-product information only—such as job orders or daily production reports—are control records. They are used primarily in the plant work areas for scheduling and planning production.

Production Orders. Figure 7.1 shows a typical job order form. This form is used by the production manager to initiate production activity. When a job is ready for production, or when the inventory of finished products needs building up, the production manager authorizes the start of work by issuing a job order. He keeps one copy and sends a copy with the necessary instructions to each department or machine operator involved in the production.

This procedure provides a means for establishing production priorities and makes it possible for all departments or operators to plan for jobs that are coming up. Each department or operator keeps a file of pending orders arranged by the expected sequence of work. The foreman or the production manager can then check from time to time and readjust the job sequence as needed. The aim, of course, is to make sure that successive operations on all orders are scheduled as efficiently as possible.

When manufacturing operations are highly mechanized and the volume of production is near capacity, machine loading is of prime importance. In such cases, an employee or group of employees may be assigned to analyze job orders and schedule the machines so as to get the maximum use from the plant's facilities.

Job Control Record. The person responsible for control of production needs some sort of record or file to show the status of all jobs in process. A typical production control record is shown as Figure 7.2.

When the production manager issues a job order, he enters the order number and other details on the job control record. In the column headed "Departments or

Job Order

Order no.__________ Date issued__________

For__________ or Stock__________
Purchaser

Scheduled completion date__________

Product description__________

No. of items__________ Drawing no.__________ Pattern no.__________

Material requisition nos.__________

Instructions:

Date completed__________

No. of good units__________

No. of defective units__________

____
Foreman or supervisor

Figure 7.1

| Job Control Record | | | | | | | | | |
Order No.	Date Issued	Job Description	No. of Items	Scheduled Completion	Purchaser or for stock	Departments or operations	Date compl.	No. of Good Items	Remarks

Figure 7.2

Operations," the numbers or other identifying codes of all departments that will work on the job are entered. As the order moves through the factory, one department after another is checked off, showing where the job stands at any time.

The job control record is thus an up-to-date running history of all production activity. It shows where the factory stands in terms of jobs, units of product, and stages of completion. It is a means of control over all work in process. Furthermore, it is a ready source of information when customers ask about their orders. The information should also be used, along with sales orders or forecasts and stock records of finished products, to determine the need for new job orders.

The form shown in Figure 7.2 is just an example. How elaborate a form is needed depends on a number of factors—the number of operations, the number of jobs in process at one time, the length of time required to finish each job, the amount of detailed information needed by management. If production operations are numerous or jobs differ greatly, it may be better to use separate control cards (filed numerically) for each job. The production order form can be used for this.

Other methods can be used to control production—blackboard and chalk, pegboard layouts, mechanical visual aids, or computers. The best method for a small manufacturer is the one he finds easy to understand and whose costs in money and time he can afford.

Daily Production Report. The daily production report (Figure 7.3) provides the data for recording job progress. The preceding day's production is checked for each department or operation and recorded on the daily production report.

If each job calls for only one unit, or very few units, the entries should show only the jobs completed by each department. If each job is made up of a large number of units and requires at least several days to complete, a more detailed record is needed. For such jobs, it is important to show the number of individual units completed by each department so that the stage of completion of each job in each department may be known.

Showing on the daily report the number of units lost, wasted, or spoiled uncovers trouble spots promptly. If necessary, future operations on the jobs in process can be rescheduled.

Order No.	Job Description	Dept.	No. of Items Finished	No. of Items Spoiled Lost, or Wasted	Remarks

Daily Production Report For _____
Date

Figure 7.3

Job-Order Instruction Card.   Job-order instruction cards help direct the movement of jobs through the plant. They also serve as a running history that can be used to trace responsibility for either substandard workmanship or exceptional efficiency.

A job-order instruction card (Figure 7.4) should be prepared before each job order is issued. This card goes to the department or employee who will work on the job first and then accompanies the job through all operations. Each employee or foreman

Job Order
Instruction Card

Job Order No. _____

Product _____

No. of units _____

Special Instructions:

Required Operations	Dept.	Date Compl.	Initial of Foreman or Operator

Figure 7.4

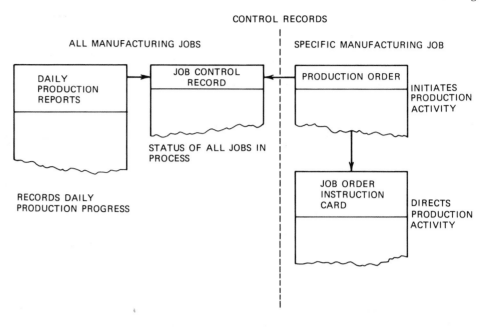

handling the job enters on the card the date his operation is completed and his initials.

Recording Job Costs

The techniques discussed so far have been solely control techniques. The forms shown in Figures 7.1 through 7.4 are in terms of units rather than dollars and cents. They tell what, how much, and where, but not how much money is involved in the units and activity. Other records are needed to gather product cost information.

For a job order plant, the four basic cost records, are the materials requisition, the job time card, the job cost record, and the production cost summary. These basic cost records should tie in with the overall accounting system. Their relation to accounts in the general or factory ledger is shown in Figure 7.5. (The numbers in the explanation that follows refer to the corresponding circled numbers in Figure 7.5.)

The *cost of materials purchased* (1) is recorded in the raw materials inventory account from vendors' invoices. The entry will read as follows:

	Debit	Credit
Raw materials inventory	x	
Accounts payable		x
To record the purchase of raw materials.		

The *materials requisition* (2) (Figure 7.6) is used to authorize all withdrawals from a storeroom or stock of raw materials. The requisitions should be prepared by someone who knows exactly what materials are needed for the job—for example, the planning department, production engineer, or production manager. Only authorized individuals should sign requisitions.

If more materials must be issued to a job already started, it may mean too much waste or spoilage. A colored requisition form for added-on issues will call attention to this possibility.

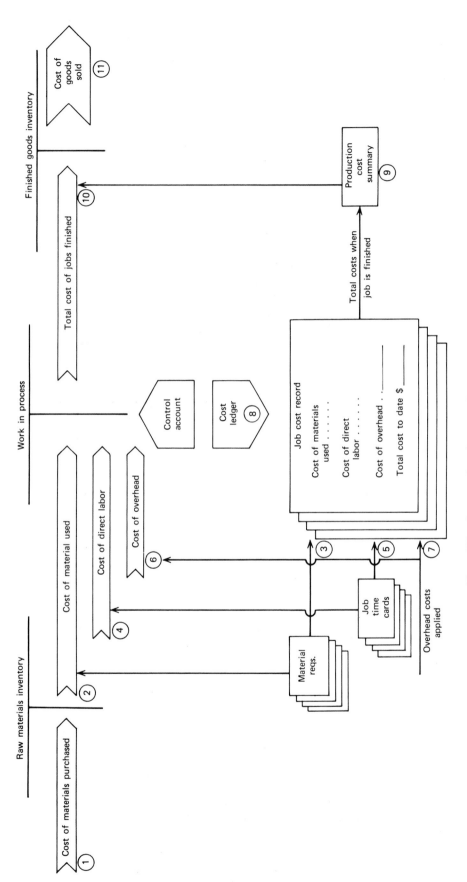

Figure 7.5. Cost records and accounts for a job-order plant.

131

The materials costs entered on the requisition are based on the unit costs shown in the raw materials inventory account. They are the basic record from which a journal entry is made to transfer costs from the raw materials inventory to the work-in-process account, as follows:

	Debit	Credit
Work in process	x	
Raw materials inventory		x
To transfer materials cost to work-in process account.		

The materials requisition is also the basic cost record for recording materials costs on the *job cost record* (3) (Figure 7.7). Direct labor and overhead costs will be added to give the total manufacturing costs of each job.

Before each production order is run, the planning department or the department foreman prepares a *job timecard* (4) (Figure 7.8) for each worker who will do any part of the job. Every time the operator starts or stops work on the job, he has his card time-stamped. When he finishes the job, the card is time-stamped again and completed. The job timecards provide information for preparing the operator's paycheck.

	Debit	Credit
Direct labor cost	x	
Accrued payroll costs		x
To record payroll costs.		

Material Requisition					
Data _____ Requisition no._____					
For _____ Production order no._____					
Department or operator					
Requested by _____					
Stores No.	Quantity Requested	Description	Quan. Issued	Unit Cost	Total Cost
Received by _____ Date _____					

Figure 7.6

A cost clerk collects the job timecards daily or weekly. He figures the labor costs and sorts the cards by job orders. Then he records the direct-labor costs (5) on the job cost record for each job on which work has been done. Some job orders may require days or even weeks in one department. When that is the case, daily job timecards may be needed to keep the job cost records current.

	Debit	Credit
Work in process—Job A	x	
Direct labor cost		x
To transfer direct labor cost to work in process		
job cost record.		

The cost of overhead (6) includes all manufacturing costs except direct materials and direct labor. These costs cannot be assigned to or identified with individual jobs, so they are applied to jobs on the basis of so much per direct labor hour or machine hour, or on some other basis.

	Debit	Credit
Accumulated overhead	x	
Rent expense		x
Utilities expense		x
Supplies		x
To transfer miscellaneous overhead expense to		
accumulated overhead clearing account.		

Once the method for distributing overhead cost has been decided, the overhead cost can be calculated for each job and entered on the job cost record. The job cost records should show the overhead rate and basis used as well as the amount applied to the job (7).

	Debit	Credit
Work in process—Job A	x	
Accumulated overhead		x
To transfer accumulated overhead to work in		
process job cost record on an allocation basis.		

On any date, the job cost record (Figure 7.7) for given job shows all the costs of the job—direct materials, direct labor, and overhead applied. All the job cost records together make up a special ledger called the *cost ledger* (8).

These costs are entered also in the work-in-process account in the general ledger. The accounting entries here are usually monthly totals from the materials requisitions, job time cards, and overhead application calculations. The work-in-process account is called a control account because its balance is always equal to the total of all costs of uncompleted jobs in the cost ledger.

It may be more convenient to use three work-in-process accounts—material-in-process, labor-in-process, and overhead-in-process—than to put all costs into a single account. But no matter how many work-in-process accounts are used, the principle is the same: When all accounting entries have been made, the total of the costs shown on the uncompleted job-cost records should equal the total costs in the work-in-process account(s).

The job-cost records are the hub of any cost system. The entries made on these forms are the end result of all the procedures used to gather cost details.

Job Cost Record

For _____ Order no. _____

Product _____ Quantity _____

Date wanted _____ Date started _____ Date completed _____

Direct Materials			Direct Labor			Applied Overhead		
Date	Req. No.	Amount	Date	Time Card No.	Amount	Basis	Rate	Amount

Summary for order no. _____

Direct materials _____

Direct labor _____

Applied overhead _____

Total factory cost _____

Factory cost per unit _____

Figure 7.7

Job Time Card

Name _____ Card no. _____

Department _____ Clock no. _____

Date	Job Order No.	Machine No.	Time Started	Time Stopped	Total Hours	Wage Rate	Total Cost

No. of pieces finished _____ Approved by _____

Figure 7.8

| | | | | Production Cost Summary for Month of _____ | | | | |
| | | | | For Department _____ | | | | |
Date Compl.	Order No.	Product	Quantity	Direct Materials	Direct Labor	Applied Overhead	Total Cost	Cost per Unit

Figure 7.9.   Production cost summary.

Just what type of job-cost records will be used depends on the types of raw materials and component parts used, the length of time required to complete each job, the number of employees doing direct labor on each job, the basis for applying overhead, the number of different overhead rates (for different operations), the degree to which the factory is departmentalized, and any special production or accounting techniques used.

The fundamental requirements, however, are always the same. There must be space for job identification, for periodic entries of direct material, direct labor, and overhead costs, and for a summary of total costs.

When a job is finished, entries are made on the *job control record* (Figure 7.2) and on a monthly *production cost summary* (9) similar to the one shown as Figure 7.9. The data for the production cost summary are taken from the summary section of the job cost record. This report is a useful source of cost information for the management of a manufacturing business.

At the end of each month or accounting period the total costs of all completed jobs, as shown on the monthly production cost summary, are entered in the journal (**10**). This journal entry transfers costs from the work-in-process account to the finished product inventory account:

	Debit	Credit
Finished product inventory	x	
Work in progress		x
To transfer costs of completed jobs to finished product inventory.		

When finished products are sold to a customer—either on special order or out of inventory—the costs of those products are taken out of the inventory account and charged to the *cost of goods sold account* (**11**). (The cost of goods sold will appear in the income statement).

COST RECORDS

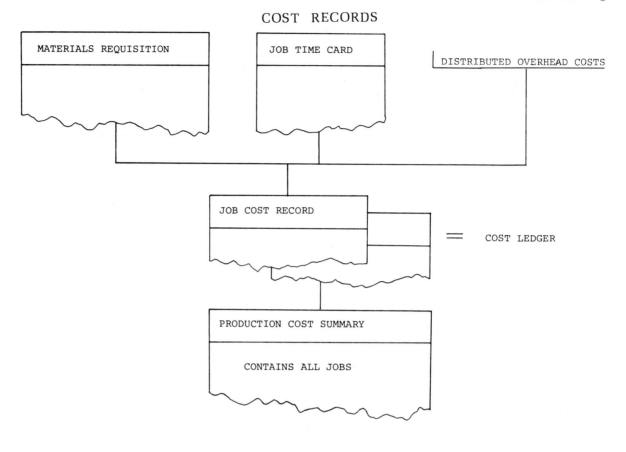

	Debit	Credit
Cost of goods sold	x	
Finished product inventory		x
To record the sale of products.		

PROCESS COSTING

In a continuous-processing plant production costs are handled by processes, operations, or activities rather than by jobs, as in a job-order system. Costs per product unit are computed by averaging costs for the output of a given time period.

Process cost accounting is suitable for four general types of manufacturing:

1. Where only one or a few products are manufactured.
2. Where repetitive, continuous processing through standardized processes is required.
3. Where there is no need to maintain the identity of individual product items.
4. Where production is for stock rather than for special orders.

```
JOB ORDER COST SYSTEM                PROCESS COST SYSTEM


Types of Manufacturers:              Types of Manufacturers:

  ● Goods produced for individual      ● One or few products are manufactured
    customer specifications
                                       ● Repetitive, continuous standardized
  ● Goods produced for a single          processing is used
    customer with frequent
    specification changes              ● Product has no individual identity

  ● Goods produced for the
    government

                                     Cost Center = Department


Cost Center = Job
                                     Divided by Cost of Individual Process

                                     Number of Units Processed
Total Manufacturing Cost Divided by

Number of product units produced
```

By classifying costs according to process or operation, a process cost system directs attention to specific areas in production. For example, in a small foundry, costs may be assigned separately for melting, coremaking, molding, and finishing operations. These groupings give management a basis for pinpointing responsibility and taking corrective action.

A process accounting system is usually less expensive and less cumbersome to operate than a job-order system. Much of the detail needed to associate costs with individual items or groups of items is unnecessary in a process sytem.

Cost-Data Detail in a Process System

In a process cost system, the cost center is a department rather than a job. Each operating department that takes part in the manufacturing process is a cost center. Costs are determined with reference to each separate process, and the extent of detail depends on the number of departments (processes) that exist as cost centers.

The amount of detail also depends on the layout and organization of the plant. In most cases, a compromise is necessary between the ideal organization from an accounting viewpoint and the practical limits imposed by the cost of recordkeeping.

Production Control

Formal job orders are not needed for control purposes in a plant in which (1) production is continuous, (2) the capacities of the various departments are well balanced, and (3) sales potential is relatively unlimited. A production budget built around expected sales volume can be used to keep general control of manufacturing activities. Such plants may include mining operations, ice plants, steam plants, and producers of staple food products.

If a perishable product is involved, however, this sort of loose production control may produce bottlenecks in some of the manufacturing processes or too large inventories of finished products. Production orders or schedules similar to those used in a job order plant may have to be used. The only function of these orders or schedules is to help control production activities. They serve no accounting function in a processing plant and are not used as a basis for assigning costs.

In any continuous processing plant, the production budget or job orders should be supplemented by production reports. Records showing quantities produced by each department each day and also monthly production summaries should be compiled as an aid to control.

These records will enable management to keep up to date on achievement within the plant. Planning for future production can then be adjusted in the light of current production levels, and per unit cost calculations for each can be made in time for any needed corrective action. The basic records can be kept by machine operators, department foremen, timekeepers, or production-planning personnel.

Characteristics of a Process Cost System

The type of process cost system to be used depends on the manufacturing techniques and the number of products made. Suppose, for example, that three different products are made (call them A, B, and C), and that each one requires a different manufacturing process. Each of the three processing departments—Process A, Process B, and Process C—is then a cost center. The costs of materials, labor, and overhead for each product are charged to the corresponding process. The costs of the finished products are then transferred to the finished goods inventory accounts. The unit cost of manufacturing the product is found by dividing the total of the costs assigned to each cost center by the number of units produced.

In another plant, a number of standardized manufacturing processes may be required to make a single product. Since the processes follow one another in sequence, the system is known as a sequential process system. For example, work on Product A begins in Process 1, continues in Process 2, and is completed in Process 3. Each of the three processing departments is a cost center.

Costs are then assigned as follows:

Process 1 is assigned the costs of materials and also its share of overhead costs.

Process 2 receives from Process 1 the partially processed product together with the costs from Process 1, and is assigned also the costs of its own materials, labor, and overhead.

Process 3 receives the further processed but still incomplete product and its costs from Process 2, and the materials, labor, and overhead costs of Process 3 are added.

The toal cost of the finished Product A is finally transferred out of Process 3 to the finished goods inventory account.

Figure 7.10 is a diagram of the flow of production costs in the process cost-accounting system of a two-product, two-process company. This company is used as an illustration throughout the rest of this chapter.

Some typical figures for a continuous-process manufacturing operation—the Hero Manufacturing Company—will be used to illustrate the points made in this chapter. Assume that this company produces two different products from similar raw materials. Each product goes through two well-defined processes in its manufacture, as shown in the cost-flow diagram. There is only one service department—the repair shop, which services and repairs machinery in all four of the producing departments.

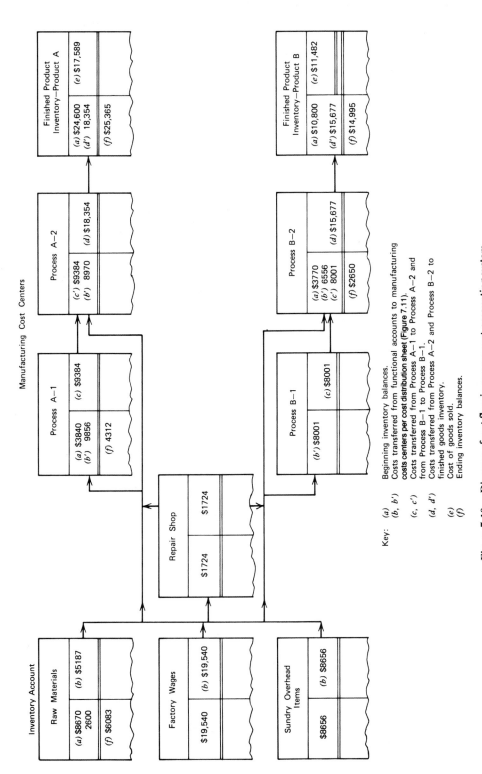

Manufacturing Cost Centers

Key:
(a)   Beginning inventory balances.
(b, b')   Costs transferred from functional accounts to manufacturing
            costs centers per cost distribution sheet (Figure 7.11).
(c, c')   Costs transferred from Process A–1 to Process A–2 and
            from Process B–1 to Process B–1.
(d, d')   Costs transferred from Process A–2 and Process B–2 to
            finished goods inventory.
(e)   Cost of goods sold.
(f)   Ending inventory balances.

Figure 7.10.   Diagram of cost flow in process cost-accounting system.

The Ledger Accounts.   Accounting for costs begins when bills are received from vendors of goods or services and payrolls are prepared. The company keeps a general ledger with accounts for the various assets, liabilities, owners' equities, revenues, and expenses. Entries are made from the bills and payrolls in a voucher register, and costs are then posted to the ledger accounts.

In a system like this (two products, each going through two processes), material and operating costs have to be assigned to the four processes. This can be done when the costs are incurred, but in most cases it is more practical to record daily and weekly entries in ledger accounts such as Wages, Supervision, Power, Insurance, Supplies, and so on. At the end of the month, these accounts are closed and the accumulated costs charged to the producing departments by means of a cost-distribution sheet.

The Cost Distribution Sheet.   Figure 7.11 shows the cost-distribution sheet prepared by the Hero Manufacturing Company at the end of each month. The method by which each cost-entry is apportioned to the process accounts is also shown.

On the cost distribution sheet, production costs are distributed to the accounts of the repair shop and the four processing departments. Adjustments made to record end-of-the-month entries such as depreciation expense, insurance, taxes, and so on are also distributed. Note that repair shop costs are first charged to the repair shop account and then reassigned to the process accounts.

Journal Entries.   Figure 7.12 shows the general journal entries made at the end of the month to record the totals from the voucher register, the weekly payrolls, and the check register. Sales journal totals and cash receipts journal totals for the month are also shown in this exhibit. The voucher register and payroll entries, together with end-of-the-month adjusting entries, are used in preparing the cost-distribution sheet. When the cost-distribution sheet has been completed, the totals are summarized in a General Journal entry, shown in Figure 7.13.

The total cost of product units completed during the month must be brought together in the finished product and cost of sales accounts. For this, the following cost transfers will be entered in the general journal:

> Work in process from Processes A-1 and B-1 to Processes A-2 and B-2 respectively.
>
> Finished products from Processes A-2 and B-2 to the corresponding finished product accounts.
>
> Costs of product units sold from the finished product accounts to the cost of sales accounts.

Before this can be done, however, it is necessary to know the cost per unit for each process and for finished product units.

Unit Cost Figures and Equivalent Units.   The total of the charges in each process account shows the production cost of the process for the month. But control of costs requires information about the cost per unit. It doesn't help much to know that the total production cost for Process A-1 in January was $9586. Whether this figure shows good or poor performance for the department depends on how many acceptable product units were produced. How does the cost per unit compare with previous costs per unit?

If no partly completed units remain in a process inventory either at the beginning or at the end of the month, the unit cost for that process can be found very easily. Simply divide the total of the charges by the number of units completed during the month.

| | | | | Accounts Debited | | | | | |
| | | | | Product A | | Product B | | | |
Entry No.	Accounts Credited	Amount of Credit	Repair Shop	Process A-1	Process A-2	Process B-1	Process B-2	Selling Expense	Administrative Expense
1	Power[1]	$220	$75	$30	$40	$30	$35	$5	$5
2	Water[1]	28	60	20					8
3	Machinery rental[2]	160				100			
4	Factory wages[3]	19,540	966	6,682	4,730	4,320	2,842		
5	Supervision[4]	750		200	300	150	100		
6	Raw materials[5]	5,187		468	1,490	1,507	1,722		
7	Supplies[6]	240	20	54		56		62	48
8	Depreciation—building[7]	740	74	148	148	148	119	29	74
9	Depreciation—machinery and equipment[8]	900	250	120	350	90	90		
10	Fire insurance[9]	100	10	20	20	16	20	6	8
11	Wages payable[10]	5,720	264	1,860	1,340	1,220	1,036		
12	Taxes payable[9]	50	5	10	10	8	10	3	4
13	Repair shop total[11]		(1,724)	244	542	356	582		
14	Allowance for doubtful accounts	150							150
15	Advertising	32						32	
16	Salesmen's salaries	948						948	
17	Sundry selling expense	380						380	
18	Executive salaries	1,200							1,200
19	Telephone	36							36
20	Sundry administrative expense	295							295
	Total	$36,676	0	$9,856	$8,970	$8,001	$6,556	$1,465	$1,828
	Equivalent units of production			320	300	210	220		
	Production cost per unit			$30.80	$29.90	$38.10	$29.80		

[1]Estimated consumption

[2]Machine-hour logs.

[3]Timecard summaries.

[4]Estimated time spent in each department.

[5]Requisition summaries.

[6]Estimated consumption.

[7]Percent of floor space.

[8]Cost of machinery and equipment.

[9]Appraised values of equipment and floor space occupied.

[10]Timecard summary since last pay period.

[11]Detailed records of time spent for each department.

Figure 7.11 Cost-distribution sheet.

	Debit	Credit
Voucher Register		
Raw materials	$ 2,600	
Supplies	376	
Payroll liability	22,648	
Power	220	
Telephone	36	
Water	28	
Machinery rental	160	
Advertising	32	
Sundry selling expense	380	
Sundry administrative expense	295	
Vouchers payable		$26,775
Payroll		
Factory wages	$19,540	
Salesmen's salaries	948	
Executives' salaries	1,200	
Superintendence	750	
Salaries payable		$22,438
Check Register		
Vouchers payable	$28,600	
Cash in bank		$28,600
Sales Journal		
Accounts receivable	$36,000	
Sales—Product A		$21,000
Sales—Product B		15,000
Cash Receipts Journal		
Cash in bank	$34,320	
Accounts receivable		$34,320

Figure 7.12   Miscellaneous General Journal entries.

	Debit	Credit
Repair shop	$1,724	
Process A-1	9,856	
Process A-2	8,970	
Process B-1	8,001	
Process B-2	6,556	
Selling expense	1,465	
Administrative expense	1,828	
Power		$ 220
Water		28
Machinery rental		160
Factory wages		19,540
Supervision		750
Allowance for doubtful accounts		150
Raw materials		5,187
Supplies		240
Allowance for depreciation of building		740
Allowance for depreciation of machinery		
and equipment		900
Unexpired fire insurance		100
Salaries payroll		5,720
Taxes payable		50
Repair shop		1,724
Advertising		32
Salesmen's salaries		948
Selling expense		380
Executives' salaries		1,200
Telephone		36
Administrative expense		295

Figure 7.13.   General Journal entry from cost-distribution sheet.

If there are inventories of work in process, the per unit cost figures must be based on the number of "equivalent units" produced. Equivalent units produced are not necessarily the same as the number of units completed and transferred to the next process. The half-completed product units in the beginning and ending inventories must also be taken into account.

In Process A-1 transferred to Process A-2. But this does not represent the total production of Process A-1 during the month. Actually, the month's production was equivalent to 320 units, as the following figures show:

Completion of 240 half-finished units in the beginning inventory	120 units
Total production of 60 units both started and finished during the period	60 units
Half-production of 280 units remaining in the ending inventory	140 units
Equivalent work units	320 units

Cost Flows.   Another factor in determining costs involves the flow of costs. At any given time, an inventory may contain identical units of quite different costs. The price of raw materials or wages may have changed, and it may not be possible to attach specific costs to specific units of product.

The best method to use for production flow is the first in first out (FIFO) method. That is, it is assumed that the first product units (and their cost) that go into a process are the first units (and costs) to be transferred to the next process.

The method used to transfer costs is important in times of fast-changing costs. It also matters if the work on each unit of product goes on for a long time. In such cases, very different cost figures may result from using cost flow methods other than FIFO.

Transfer Entries in the General Journal.   Both the equivalent unit and the cost flow concepts are used in preparing the entries that transfer costs through the various steps from the first manufacturing process to cost of sales.

Process A-1 Costs.   The total cost of the month's production in Process A-1, as shown on the cost distribution sheet (Figure 7.11) was $9856. The number of equivalent units, as figured above, was 320. The January *cost per equivalent unit* in Process A-1, then, was $9856 divided by 320, or $30.80. The cost of the 280 units in the ending inventory (140 equivalent units) is 140 times $30.80, or $4312.

The cost of the 300 units completed in Process A-1 and sent on to Process 2 must be figured differently. Using the first-in first-out method, you assume that the units transferred include the beginning inventory at December costs. So the cost of the 300 units sent to Process 2 is figured as follows:

Beginning inventory of 240 units (120 equivalent units) carried forward from December	$3840
Completion of these units at January costs (120 times $30.80)	3969
60 units produced entirely in January (60 times $30.80)	1848
Total cost of the 300 units transferred from Process A-1 to Process A-2	$9384

The first item in Figure 7.14 shows the general journal entry made to transfer this cost from Process A-1 to Process A-2.

Process A-2 Costs.   Process A-2 requires only a few minutes for each unit of Product A. The department is able to handle the output of Process A-1 as it comes in, so there is no beginning nor ending inventory in Process A-2.

During January, the 300 units completed in Process A-1 were made into the finished Product A at a total additional cost of $8970, giving a total of $18,826 for phases A-1 and A-2, a cost per unit of $61.18. A general journal entry is made to transfer the cost of the completed units from process A-2 to the Finished Product A account. This is the second entry in Figure 7.14.

Product A Sales.   The sales records show that 286 units of Product A were sold during January and that 414 units are on hand at the end of January. The finished product inventory account at the beginning of the month showed 400 units at a total cost of $24,600. This figure comes out to $61.50 per unit.

Again, the FIFO method of transferring costs is used, and the 286 units sold are assumed to have come from the 400-unit beginning inventory. The cost of sales is therefore based on the $61.50 cost per unit, and the total cost of the 286 units is $17,589.

The third entry in Figure 7.14 shows the general journal entry transferring this cost from the finished Product A account to cost of sales.

	Debit	Credit
Process A-2	$ 9,384	
Process A-1		$ 9,384
To transfer cost of 300 product units finished in process A-1.		
Finished Product A	18,354	
Process A-2		18,354
To transfer cost of 300 finished product units to finished product inventory.		
Cost of sales—Product A	17,589	
Finished Product A		17,589
To transfer cost of 286 units sold from finished product account.		
Process B-2	8,001	
Process B-1		8,001
To transfer cost of 210 product units finished in process B-1.		
Finished Product B	15,677	
Process B-2		15,677
To transfer cost of 230 units of finished product to finished product inventory.		
Cost of sales—Product B	11,482	
Finished Product B		11,482
To transfer cost of 170 units sold from finished product account.		

Figure 7.14   General Journal entries to transfer costs.

Product B.   The costs for Product B are handled in the same way as those for Product A, as described above. The general journal entries are shown in Figure 7.14 following those for Product A.

If All Materials Are Added at the Start of a Process.   In this chapter, it has been assumed that all labor, materials, and overhead are added evenly throughout each process. This is usually the case with labor and overhead. In some operations, however, all the materials have to be put into production at the beginning of a process.

For example, it is estimated that the product units in the ending work-in-process inventory for Process A-1 are half-completed. This means that materials and other production costs for those units come to one-half the amount necessary to complete them.

Suppose, however, that all materials have to be added in Process A-1 at the beginning of the process. Materials costs would then have to be separated from other production costs. If unit costs for Process A-1 are $1.40 for materials and $30 for labor and overhead, the cost of the ending inventory of 280 units would be figured like this:

Materials in process (280 units at $1.40)	$ 392
Labor and overhead in process (280 units at $15)	4200
Cost of ending inventory (280 units complete as to materials and ½ complete as to labor and overhead)	$4592

Lost or Spoiled Units of Product.   In the illustration, it was assumed that each unit of material became one unit of finished product. However, manufacturing processes often involve shrinkage as a result of evaporation, spoilage, breakage, pilferage, and so on.

If the shrinkage is an unavoidable result of the producing activity, the costs of lost units should be distributed over the remaining product units, both those completed at the end of the period and those in the ending work-in-process inventory.

If, on the other hand, the amount of shrinkage varies because of variations in operating efficiency, the cost of lost units should be recorded in separate accounts for each department. These account balances then provide direct information about production efficiency.

Chapter Eight

Pensions and Executive Compensation

A HISTORY

It is necessary to plan for your financial security and that of your employees through pensions, profit sharing, and executive compensation. In 1974 Congress passed a significant piece of pension legislation. Regulations interpreting this legislation are only now becoming fully understood by accountants, lawyers, and others who work in the area of compensation.

The Pension Reform Act of 1974, officially designated as the "Employee Retirement Income Security Act of 1974" (ERISA), has been described as a landmark piece of legislation in the area of employee economic security. The intention of the Act was to insure that pension plans are financed and operated in such a manner that employees actually receive benefits promised to them.

The Social Security Act of 1935 was the first major employee benefit legislation. Prior to the Social Security Act old age survivors and disability insurance benefits were primarily limited to governmental pension plans and a few voluntary private plans.

The growth of labor unions also had an impact on the development of private benefit plans. The Taft-Hartley Act of 1947 amended previous legislation concerning the conduct of labor management negotiations. A section of that legislation provided for joint administration of plans, and restrictions on the use of contributions to such plans. In 1949, a court decision involving Inland Steel firmly established that the terms of a pension plan are subject to mandatory collective bargaining. Unions have been active in pension plans since that time.

In 1958 Congress passed the Welfare and Pension Plans Disclosure Act which provided for the filing of a plan description and an annual report form for employee benefit plans.

In 1974, ERISA greatly expanded governmental involvement in employee benefit plans. While ERISA does not require an employer to establish or maintain a plan, it provides for certain minimum standards for participation, vesting and funding, expanded trustee responsibility and disclosure requirements, and termination insurance if the employer goes out of business. In addition, the Act provided for governmental agencies to interpret and enforce the law. Most pension and profit sharing plans have had to be amended as a result of ERISA.

Prior to ERISA, an employer was able to design a pension or profit sharing plan with strict eligibility and vesting provisions. (Vesting is defined as the right to receive pension benefits regardless of whether an employee continues working.) Technically vesting was not required prior to normal retirement age. However, anti-discrimination rulings and collective bargaining resulted in earlier vesting and other benefits. ERISA established minimum age and service requirements and minimum formulas for vesting.

The Act also established minimum funding standards for pension plans. Prior to ERISA, unfunded plans were allowed to exist. The benefits paid under unfunded plans were entirely dependent on the continued existence and earnings of the employer. ERISA provides that if you establish a pension plan, you must set aside cash funds each year sufficient to pay the future pensions earned during that year.

The amount of cash required to be contributed in any year to a pension plan is generally based on actuarial valuations prior to ERISA.

For example, you may adopt a pension plan in 1980, but because your company has been in business since 1972, you already have a liability for past service of your employees.

The minimum funding now required under ERISA specifies that the past service liability must be funded over a period of years, typically a maximum of 30.

ERISA established the Pension Benefit Guaranty Corporation, which is to make up deficiencies if a pension plan terminates with insufficient assets to pay benefits that are vested. Employers can be contingently liable for up to 30% of their net worth for any deficiency in the assets of a terminated plan.

A participant under a pension plan is defined as an employee or former employee, or other beneficiary who is or may become eligible to receive a benefit of any type from an employee benefit plan. Generally, an employee cannot be excluded from a plan because of age or service if he or she is at least 25 years old and has completed at least one year of service. The one year of service requirement may be extended to three years if full and immediate vesting is provided. A year of service is defined as a 12 month period in which the employee has worked at least 1000 hours.

A defined contribution retirement plan cannot exclude an employee because he is too old at the time of his employment. However, a defined benefit plan can exclude employees who start employment within five years of normal retirement.

Pension plans may be classified into two primary categories—defined benefit plans and defined contribution plans.

Defined benefit plans provide a definitely determinable retirement benefit when an employee reaches retirement age.

Defined contribution plans, on the other hand, provide for an individual account for each participant and for benefits based solely on the amount contributed to the participant's account, and any income, expenses, gains and losses, and any forfeitures from accounts of other participants which may be allocated to the participant's account.

Pension plan benefits are usually paid out in the form of a life annuity beginning at a person's normal retirement age. Other methods of paying benefits include installment payments and lump sum distributions.

Contributions to a defined benefit plan are based on actuarial calculations designed to estimate the amount necessary to fund the payment of specified pension benefits to be paid at retirement.

Under a defined contribution plan, the rate of contribution is either fixed (usually a percentage of annual salary or a percentage of company profits), or it may be determined on a discretionary basis by the management of the company.

VESTED BENEFITS

Vested benefits are benefits that are not dependent on the employee continuing in the service of an employer. In other words, vesting means that an employee's rights to accrued benefits are not forfeitable, even if he or she terminates employment.

ERISA requires that a vesting plan meet one of the following minimum vesting rules:

1. *Ten year service rule*—100% vesting after 10 years of service.
2. *Graded 5 to 15 year service rule*—25% vesting after 5 years of service, 5% additional vesting for each year of service from year 6 through 10, 10% additional vesting for each year of service from year 11 through year 15, so that an employee is 100% vested after 15 years.
3. "*Rule of 45*"—50% vesting when the sum of an employee's age and years of service total 45—if he or she has completed at least 5 years of service—and 10% additional vesting for each year of service thereafter. Additionally, a participant under the "Rule of 45" must be 50% vested after 10 years of service, 60% after 11 years, and so on, so that an employee is at least 50% vested after 10 years and 100% vested after 15 years regardless of his or her age.

PRUDENT MAN RULE

ERISA defines a person to be a fiduciary under a pension plan. A fiduciary must be guided in his conduct by the prudent man rule. This rule requires "care, skill, prudence, and diligence under the circumstances then prevailing that a prudent man acting in a like capacity and familiar with such matters would use in the conduct of an enterprise of a like character with like aims."* Furthermore, a fiduciary is required to diversify the investments of a plan so as to minimize the risk of large loss.

PENSION PLAN INVESTMENTS

Certain types of investments for pension plans are limited or even prohibited.

Defined benefit plans cannot invest more than 10% of plan assets in *employer securities* or *employer real estate*. Defined contribution plans can invest more than 10% of their assets in employer securities if that is the explicit intention of the plan. However, a defined contribution plan cannot invest more than 10% of its assets in employer real estate. The definition of employer real estate is a building that is owned by the pension plan and is leased to the employer.

Fiduciaries are prohibited from engaging directly or indirectly in certain transactions with a *party-in-interest*. A party-in-interest is defined as the employer, the union, persons rendering service to the plan, officers and employees of the plan, or relatives of any of the foregoing.

The prohibited transactions include:

1. A sale, exchange or lease of property between the plan and a party-in-interest.
2. A loan or extension of credit between the plan and a party-in-interest.

*Pension Reform Act, 1974, Section 404.

3. The furnishing of goods, services, or facilities between the plan and a party-in-interest.

4. A transfer of plan assets to a party-in-interest or a transfer for the use or benefit of a party-in-interest.

5. An acquisition of employer securities or real estate in violation of the provisions of the Act relating to the 10% limitation discussed above.

PENSION PAYMENTS

Pension benefits can be paid in one of two ways: (1) as a lump-sum distribution, or (2) as an annuity.

A *lump-sum distribution* is a payment of the entire balance due to an employee within one taxable year. Normally this would be because of death, or separation from service prior to normal retirement age. However, a lump-sum payment may be made any time after age $59\frac{1}{2}$.

Any amounts of the lump-sum distribution contributed by the employee are not taxed.

The recipient of a lump-sum distribution may elect a ten year averaging rule. The rule works this way:

1. *Figure the taxable portion of the lump-sum distribution.* For example, assume the lump-sum distribution is $50,000 and that $10,000 of this was contributed by the employee. The taxable portion would be $40,000.

2. *Subtract a "minimum distribution allowance" from the taxable portion.* (The minimum distribution allowance is one half of the first $20,000 of the taxable portion of the lump-sum distribution. If the taxable portion is more than $20,000, the minimum distribution allowance must be reduced by 20% of the excess.)

   For example, if the taxable portion is $40,000, the minimum distribution allowance would be one half of $20,000—or $10,000—except that this must be reduced by 20% of the excess above $20,000 (20% of $20,000) or $4000. Therefore, the minimum distribution allowance is $6000 ($10,000 − $4000). The taxable portion of the lump-sum distribution is now $40,000 less $6000 or $34,000.

3. *Compute tax on $2200 plus one tenth of the figure obtained in Step 2 above, and multiply by 10.* (Use the tax rate table for single individuals.) For example, the tax is based on $2200 + $3400 or $5600. The tax on this amount is $376. Multiplied by 10 this equals $3760.

4. *Multiply the tax obtained in Step 3 above by a ratio obtained by dividing the number of months of participation in a pension plan after January 1, 1974 by the total number of months of participation under the plan.* (This number will be added to another taxes payable). For example, the recipient of the $50,000 lump-sum distribution retires on December 31, 1980 after being employed and participating in a pension plan for 20 years. The number of months from January 1, 1974 to December 31, 1980 is 84. The total number of months in 20 years is 240. Therefore $1316 [($^{84}/_{240}$) × $3760] would be the ordinary income portion of the tax on the lump-sum distribution.

5. *Multiply the taxable portion of the lump sum distribution by one minus the fraction obtained in Step 4 above.* (This amount is considered a long term

capital gain.) For example, the taxable portion of the lump-sum distribution, $40,000, is multiplied by $^{156}/_{240}$. This amount, $26,000, is included in taxable income as a long-term capital gain (usually taxable at a maximum of 28%).

An *annuity* is taxed as ordinary income in the year the payment is received. The payment represents income that has not been previously taxed to the recipient. For example, assume the $50,000 lump-sum distribution discussed above will be paid in 10 equal installments over 10 years. Each year the recipient would get $5000, and of this $4000 [($40,000/$50,000) $\times$ 5000] would be taxed.

SELF-EMPLOYED PENSION PLANS

Congress has provided that if you are self-employed, or if you work for a company that does not have a pension plan, you may create your own plan. This plan is called a Keogh Plan. For persons who work for a company that does not have a pension plan, the Individual Retirement Account (IRA) is available.

Under the Self-Employed Individuals Tax Retirement Act of 1962, self-employed individuals can be covered under qualified retirement plans, known as HR-10 plans or Keogh Plans. The qualification requirements for a Keogh Plan are similar to the requirements for a corporate retirement plan. However, the requirements for qualification are more stringent where a Keogh Plan covers an "owner-employee" (an individual who derives income from an unincorporated business and who is also a proprietor or a partner who owns more than 10% of the capital).

ERISA increased the maximum deductible contributions a self-employed individual can make to a qualified plan to 15% of earned income, up to $7500 per year. In applying the $7500 deduction limitation, the self-employed person can count only the first $100,000 of earned income. This means that he must contribute to the plan at a rate of 7.5% of compensation for both himself and his employees in order to achieve the $7500 limitation. The limitation is also applicable to shareholder employees of Sub-Chapter S corporations.

Individual Retirement Accounts

An employee who is not an active participant in any qualified pension, profit-sharing, stock bonus, or annuity plan is entitled to set up his own retirement plan. Annual contributions in cash up 15% of compensation or $15,000, whichever is less, may be made to an individual retirement account and deducted from an employee's gross income.

Earnings on IRAs are accumulated tax free and distribution may be made after age $59\frac{1}{2}$. IRAs cannot purchase life insurance as an investment, but annuitites are permissible.

STOCK OPTIONS

One form of executive compensation common in the past is the stock option plan. Because of the Tax Reform Act of 1976, which eliminated most of the favorable aspects of stock option plans, and because of the lackluster performance of the stock market in recent years, stock option plans have fallen into disfavor.

However, there are some types of stock options or pseudo stock options that are still being used.

In general, if a company grants a stock option to an employee, the employee recognizes income, and the company receives a deduction for the difference between the fair market value of the stock and the option price.

Example. If an employee is granted an option to purchase 100 shares of stock at $5 per share and the market value of the stock at the date of the grant is $8 per share, then the employee has taxable income, and the company is entitled to a compensation paid deduction of $300 [$(8 - 5) \times 100$]. If the stock has no market value, or if the option is highly restricted as how it may be exercised then the recognition of taxable income may be deferred until the restrictions lapse or the option is exercised.

Because of the taxable nature of stock options, many companies are considering the adoption of so-called "tandem" stock option and stock appreciation rights plans.

Many companies would like to provide employees the economic benefits inherent in stock option arrangements. However, the Tax Reform Act of 1976 eliminated the formerly favorable tax treatment of qualified stock options. For this reason, and to eliminate some of the risks involved in holding shares after exercise of an option and to make it unnecessary for employees to incur debt to finance the exercise of options, many companies have supplied their option plans with *stock appreciation rights*.

Stock appreciation rights are rights granted to employees to receive the excess of the market value per share of stock above a stipulated price either in cash, in stock, or in some combination of both.

A tandem plan provides that a stock appreciation right and a stock option are granted simultaneously, and may be exercised by the employee over a certain length of time. The exercise of the option cancels the stock appreciation right and vice versa. This dual nature of the plan allows the employee to choose the features that best suit his or her tax situation and anticipation with respect to future appreciation of the stock.

Appendix One

Business Plan for Small Manufacturers

SUMMARY

A business plan can provide the owner-manager or prospective owner-manager of a small manufacturing firm with a pathway to profit. This *Aid* is designed to help an owner-manager in drawing up his business plan.

In building a pathway to profit you need to consider the following questions: What business am I in? What goods do I sell? Where is my market? Who will buy? Who is my competition? What is my sales strategy? What merchandising methods will I use? How much money is needed to operate my company? How will I get the work done? What management controls are needed? How can they be carried out? When should I revise my plan? Where can I go for help?

No one can answer such questions for you. As the owner-manager you have to answer them and draw up *your* business plan. The pages of this *Aid* are a combination of text and workspaces so you can write in the information you gather in developing *your* business plan—a logical progression from a commonsense starting point to a commonsense ending point.

FIRST PRINTED JULY 1973

A NOTE ON USING THIS AID

It takes time and energy and patience to draw up a satisfactory business plan. Use this **Aid** to get your ideas and the supporting facts down on paper. And, above all, make changes in your plan on these pages as that plan unfolds and you see the need for changes.

Bear in mind that anything you leave out of the picture will create an additional cost, or drain on your money, when it unexpectedly crops up later on. If you leave out or ignore enough items, your business is headed for disaster.

Keep in mind, too, that your final goal is to put your plan into action. More will be said about this step near the end of this **Aid.**

WHAT'S IN THIS FOR ME?

Time was when an individual could start a small business and prosper provided he was strong enough to work long hours and had the knack for selling for more than the raw materials or product cost him. Small stores, grist mills, livery stables, and blacksmith shops sprang up in many crossroad communities as Americans applied their energy and native intelligence to settling the continent.

Today this native intelligence is still important. But by itself the common sense for which Americans are famous will not insure success in a small business. Technology, the marketplace, and even people themselves have become more complicated than they were 100, or even 25, years ago.

Common sense must be combined with new techniques in order to succeed in the space age. Just as one would not think of launching a manned space capsule without a flight plan, so one should not think of launching a new small manufacturing business without a business plan.

A business plan is an exciting new tool which the owner-manager of a small business can use to plot a "course" for his company. Such a plan is a logical progression from a commonsense starting point to a commonsense ending point.

To build a business plan for his company, an owner-manager needs only to think and react as a manager to questions such as: What product is to be manufactured? How can it best be made? What will it cost me? Who will buy the product? What profit can I make?

WHY AM I IN BUSINESS?

If you're like most businessmen, you're in business to make money and be your own boss. But, few businessmen would be able to say that those are the only reasons. The money that you will make from your business will seldom seem like enough for all the long hours, hard work, and responsibility that go along with being the boss.

Then, why do so many stay in business?

This is hardly the time for philosophy. If you're starting or expanding a business, you have enough to think about. But, whether or not you even think about it, the way you operate your business will reflect your "business philosophy."

Consider this. An owner-manager inspects a production run and finds a minor defect. Even though in nine out of ten cases the user of his product would not notice the defect, the owner decides to scrap the entire run.

What does this tell about his philosophy? It shows that he gets an important reward from doing what he feels is the right thing—in this case, providing a quality product.

The purpose of this section is not to play down the importance of making a profit. Profits are important. They will keep your business going and attract additional capital into your business. But you should be aware that there are other rewards and responsibilities associated with having your own business.

In your planning, you might give some thought to your responsibilities to your employees, your community, your stockholders, your customers, your product, and profit. Jot these down. Later, when you've lined-up your management team, discuss this subject with them. This type of group thinking will help everyone, including yourself, understand the basic purposes for each day's work.

Even though you won't advertise it throughout your market, the way you operate your business will reflect your business philosophy.

WHAT BUSINESS AM I IN?

In making your business plan, the next question to consider is: What business am I really in? At first reading, this question may seem silly. "If there is one thing I know," you say to yourself, "it is what business I'm in." But hold on. Some owner-managers go broke and others waste their savings because they are confused about the business they are really in.

The experience of an old line manufacturing company provides an example of dealing with the question: What business am I really in? In the early years of this century, the founder of the company had no trouble answering the question. As he put it, "I make and sell metal trash cans." This answer held true for his son until the mid-1950's when sales began to drop off. After much thought, the son decided he was in the container business.

Based on this answer, the company dropped several of its lines of metal trash cans, modified other lines, and introduced new products, such as shipping cartons used by other manufacturers and Government agencies.

What business am I in? (Write your answer here) _____

_____   _____

_____   _____

_____   _____

Asking questions like: What does my product do for my customer? Why? When? Where? How? What doesn't it do? What should it do later but doesn't now? can lead to the ultimate conclusion on what business you're in and possibly direct you to new lines of products or enterprises.

MARKETING

When you have decided what business you're really in, you have just made your first marketing decision. Now you must face other marketing considerations.

Successful marketing starts with you, the owner-manager. You have to know your product, your market, your customers, and your competition.

Before you plan production, you have to decide who your market is, where it is, why they will buy your product, whether it is a growth or static market, if there are any seasonal aspects of the market, and what percentage of the market you will shoot for in the first, second, and third year of operation. Your production goals and plans must be based on and be responsive to this kind of fact finding (market feasibility and research).

The narrative and work blocks that follow are designed to help you work out a marketing plan. Your objective is to determine what needs to be done to bring in sales dollars.

In some directories, marketing information is listed according to the Standard Industrial Classification (SIC) of the product and industry. The SIC classifies firms by the type of activity they're engaged in, and it is used to promote the uniformity and comparability of statistical data relating to market research. When you begin your market research, you may find it useful to have already classified your products according to this code. (The *Standard Industrial Classification Manual* is available from the Superintendent of Documents, U.S. Government Printing Office, Washington, D.C. 20402, for $4.50. It may also be available at your local library.)

Product   SIC No.

1. _____   _____

2. _____   _____

MARKET AREA. Where and to whom are you going to sell your product. Describe the market area you will serve in terms of geography and customer profile:

_____

_____

_____

WHO ARE YOUR COMPETITORS? List your principal competitors selling in your market area, estimate their percentage of market penetration and dollar sales in that market, and estimate their potential loss of sales as a result of your entry into the market

Name of Competitor and Location	% Share of Market	Estimated Sales	Estimated Sales He Will Lose Because of You
1. _____	_____	$_____	_____
2. _____	_____	$_____	_____
3. _____	_____	$_____	_____

HOW DO YOU RATE YOUR COMPETITION? Try to find out the strengths and weaknesses of each competitor. Then write your opinion of each of your principal competitors, his principal products, facilities, marketing characteristics, and new product development or adaptability to changing market conditions.

_____

_____

_____

Have any of your competitors recently closed operations or have they withdrawn from your market area? (State reasons if you know them):

_____   _____

_____   _____

_____   _____

_____   _____

ADVANTAGES OVER COMPETITORS. On what basis will you be able to capture your projected share of the market? Below is a list of characteristics which may indicate the advantages your product(s) enjoy over those offered by competitors. Indicate those advantages by placing a check in the proper space. If there is more than one competitor, you may want to make more than one checklist. Attach these to the worksheet.

Analyze each characteristic. For example, a higher price may not be a disadvantage if the product is of higher quality than your competitor's. You may want to make a more detailed analysis than is presented here. If you wish to spell out the specifics of each characteristic and explain where your product is disadvantaged and how this will be overcome, attach it to this worksheet. Also, the unique characteristics of your product can be the basis for advertising and sales promotion.

Remember, the more extensive your planning, the more your business plan will help you.

Product(s)	Product No. 1	Product No. 2
Price _____	( )	( )
Performance _____	( )	( )
Durability _____	( )	( )
Versatility _____	( )	( )
Speed or accuracy _____	( )	( )
Ease of operation or use _____	( )	( )
Ease of maintenance or repair _____	( )	( )
Ease or cost of installation _____	( )	( )
Size or weight _____	( )	( )
Styling or appearance _____	( )	( )
Other characteristics not listed:		
_____	( )	( )
_____	( )	( )
_____	( )	( )
_____	( )	( )
_____	( )	( )
_____	( )	( )

What, if anything, is unique about your product? _____

_____

_____

DISTRIBUTION. How will you get your product to the ultimate consumer? Will you sell it directly through your own sales organization or indirectly through middle-men, such as manufacturer's agents, brokers, wholesalers, and so on. (Use the blank to write a brief statement of your method of distribution and/or manner of sales):

_____

_____

_____

What will this method of distribution cost you? _____

_____

_____

Do you plan to use special marketing, sales, or merchandising techniques? Describe them here:

_____

_____

_____

List your customers by name, the total dollar amount they buy from you, and the amount they spend for each of your products.

Names of Principal Customers	Total Purchasing Volume	By Products	% of Your Sales
_____	_____	_____	_____
_____	_____	_____	_____
_____	_____	_____	_____
_____	_____	_____	_____

MARKET TRENDS. What has been the sales trend in your market area for your principal product(s) over the last 5 years? What do you expect it to be 5 years from now? You should indicate the source of your data and the basis of your projections.* Industry and product statistics are usually indicated in dollars. Units, such as numbers of customers, numbers of items sold, etc., may be used, but also relate your sales to dollars.

Product	Source of Data	Sales 5 Years Ago	Current Sales	Projected Sales in 5 Years
1. _____	_____	_____	_____	_____
2. _____	_____	_____	_____	_____

* This is a marketing research problem. It will require you to do some digging in order to come up with a market projection. Trade associations will probably be your most helpful source of information. The Bureau of Census publishes a great deal of useful statistics (see For Further Information). There are also the following free SBA publications to help you get started: MA187, "Using Census Data in Small Plant Marketing;" MA 192, "Profile Your Customers to Expand Industrial Sales;" SBB9, "Marketing Research Procedures;" and SBB13, "National Directories for Use in Marketing."

List the name and address of trade associations which serve your industry and indicate whether or not you are a member.

_____ _____

_____ _____

_____ _____

_____ _____

List the name and address of other organizations, governmental agencies, industry associations, etc., from which you intend to obtain management, technical, economic, or other types of information and assistance.

_____ _____

_____ _____

_____ _____

_____ _____

SHARE OF THE MARKET. What percentage of total sales in your market area do you expect to obtain for your products after your facility is in full operation?

Products or Products Category	Local Market (%)	Total Market (%)
_____	_____	_____
_____	_____	_____
_____	_____	_____

SALES VOLUME. What sales volume do you expect to reach with your products?

	Total Sales	Product(s) 1	Product(s) 2
First Year	$_____	$_____	$_____
Units	_____	_____	_____
Second Year	$_____	$_____	$_____
Units	_____	_____	_____
Third Year	$_____	$_____	$_____
Units	_____	_____	_____

PRODUCTION

Production is the work that goes on in a factory that results in a product. In making your business plan, you have to consider all the activities that are involved in turning raw materials into finished products. The work blocks which follow are designed to help you determine what production facilities and equipment you need.

MANUFACTURING OPERATIONS. List the basic operations, for example, cut and sew, machine and assemble, etc., which are needed in order to make your product.

_____   _____

_____   _____

_____   _____

RAW MATERIALS. What raw materials or components will you need, and where will you get them?

Material/Component	Source	Price	Comments (location, delivery, financing, etc.)
_____	_____	$_____	_____
_____	_____	$_____	_____
_____	_____	$_____	_____
_____	_____	$_____	_____
_____	_____	$_____	_____

What amount of raw materials and/or components will you need to stock? _____

_____

Are there any special considerations concerning the storage requirements of your raw materials? For example, will you use chemicals which can only be stored for a short time before they lose their potency?

_____

_____

EQUIPMENT.   List the equipment needed to perform the manufacturing operations. Indicate whether you will rent or buy the equipment and the cost to you.

Equipment	Buy	Rent	Your Cost
_____	_____	_____	_____
_____	_____	_____	_____
_____	_____	_____	_____

Your equipment, facilities, and method of operation must comply with the Occupational Safety and Health Act of 1970. You may obtain a copy of *Standards for General Industry* from the Superintendent of Documents, U. S. Government Printing Office, Washington, D. C. 20402, or a field office of the Occupational Safety and Health Administration for 20 cents.

LABOR SKILLS.   List the labor skills needed to run the equipment:

Skill Classification	Number of Persons Needed	Pay Rate	Availability
_____	_____	_____	_____
_____	_____	_____	_____
_____	_____	_____	_____
_____	_____	_____	_____

List the indirect labor, for example material handlers, stockmen, janitors, and so on, that is needed to keep the plant operating:

Skill Classification	Number of Persons Needed	Pay Rate	Availability
_____	_____	_____	_____
_____	_____	_____	_____
_____	_____	_____	_____
_____	_____	_____	_____

If persons with these skills are not already on your payroll, where will you get them?

_____

_____

_____

SPACE.   How much space will you need to make the product? Include restrooms, storage space for raw material and for finished products, and employee parking facilities if appropriate. Are there any local ordinances you must comply with?

_____

_____

_____

Do you own this space?	Yes_____	No_____
Will you buy this space?	Yes_____	No_____
Will you lease this space?	Yes_____	No_____
How much will it cost you?	_____	

OVERHEAD.   List the overhead items which will be needed in addition to indirect labor and include their cost. Examples are: tools, supplies, utilities, office help, telephone, payroll taxes, holidays, vacations, and salaries for your key men (sales manager, plant manager, and foremen).

_____

_____

_____

_____

HOW MUCH MONEY IS NEEDED?

Money is a tool you use to make your plan work. Money is also a measuring device. You will measure your plan in terms of dollars, and outsiders, such as bankers and other lenders, will do the same.

When you determine how much money is needed to start (or expand) your business, you can decide whether to move ahead. If the cost is greater than the profits which the business can make, there are two things to consider. Many businesses do not show a profit until the second or third year of operation. If this looks like the case with your business, you will need the plans and financial reserves to carry you through this period. On the other hand, maybe you would be better off putting your money into stocks, bonds, or other reliable investments rather than taking on the time consuming job of managing a small business.

If you are like most businessmen, your new business or expansion will require a loan. The burden of proof in borrowing money is upon the borrower. You have to show the banker or other lender how the borrowed money will be spent. Even more important, he needs to know how and when you will repay the loan.

To determine whether your plan is economically feasible, you need to pull together three sets of figures:

(1)   Expected sales and expense figures for 12 months.
(2)   Cash flow figures for 12 months.
(3)   Current balance sheet figures.

Then visit your banker. Remember, your banker or lender is your friend not your enemy. So, meet with him regularly. Share all the information and data you possess with him. If he is to really help you, he needs to know not only your strengths but also your weaknesses.

EXPECTED SALES AND EXPENSE FIGURES.   To determine whether your business can make its way in the market place, you should estimate your sales and expenses for 12 months. The form which follows is designed to help you in this task.

CASH FLOW FIGURES.   Estimates of future sales will not pay an owner-manager's bills. Cash must flow into the business at the proper times if bills are to be paid and a profit realized at the end of the year. To determine whether your projected sales and expense figures are realistic, you should prepare a cash flow forecast for the 12 months covered by your estimates of sales and expenses.

The form that follows was designed to help you estimate your cash situation and to get the appropriate figures on paper.

PROJECTED STATEMENT OF SALES AND EXPENSES FOR ONE YEAR *

	TOTAL	JAN	FEB	MAR	APR	MAY	JUN	JUL	AUG	SEP	OCT	NOV	DEC
A. Net Sales													
B. Cost of Goods Sold													
1. Raw Materials													
2. Direct Labor													
3. Manufacturing Overhead													
Indirect Labor													
Factory, Heat, Light, and Power													
Insurance and Taxes													
Depreciation													
C. Gross Margin (Subtract B from A)													
D. Selling and Administrative Expenses													
4. Salaries and Commissions													
5. Advertising Expenses													
6. Miscellaneous Expenses													
E. Net Operating Profit (Subtract D from C)													
F. Interest Expense													
G. Net Profit before Taxes (Subtract F from E)													
H. Estimated Income Tax													
I. Net Profit after Income Tax (Subtract H from G)													

* Format adapted from SBMS No. 15, *A Handbook of Small Business Finance*.
See "For Further Information."

ESTIMATED CASH FORECAST

	JAN	FEB	MAR	APR	MAY	JUN	JUL	AUG	SEP	OCT	NOV	DEC
(1) Cash in Bank (Start of Month)												
(2) Petty Cash (Start of Month)												
(3) Total Cash (add (1) and (2))												
(4) Expected Accounts Receivable												
(5) Other Money Expected												
(6) Total Receipts (add (4) and (5))												
(7) Total Cash and Receipts (add (3) and (6))												
(8) All Disbursements (for month)												
(9) Cash Balance at End of Month in Bank Account and Petty Cash (subtract (8) from (7))*												

* This balance is your starting cash balance for the next month.

CURRENT BALANCE SHEET FIGURES.   A balance sheet shows the financial conditions of a business as of a certain date. It lists what a business has, what it owes, and the investment of the owner. A balance sheet enables you to see at a glance your assets and liabilities.

Use the blanks below to draw up a current balance sheet for your company.

CURRENT BALANCE SHEET

for

_____

(name of your company)

as of

_____

(date)

ASSETS		LIABILITIES	
CURRENT ASSETS		**CURRENT LIABILITES**	
Cash	$_____	Accounts Payable	$_____
Accounts Receivable	_____	Accrued Expenses	_____
Inventory	_____	Short Term Loans	_____
FIXED ASSETS		**FIXED LIABILITIES**	
Land	$_____	Long Term Loan	$_____
Building $_____		Mortgage	_____
Equipment _____			
Total _____		NET WORTH	$_____
Less Depreciation _____	$_____		
TOTAL _____		TOTAL	$_____

GETTING THE WORK DONE

Your manufacturing business is only part way home when you have planned your marketing and production. Organization is needed if your plant is to produce what you expect it to produce.

Organization is essential because you as the owner-manager probably cannot do all the work. In which case, you'll have to delegate work, responsibility, and authority. A helpful tool in getting this done is the organization chart. It shows at a glance who is responsible for the major activities of a business. However, no matter how your operation is organized, keep control of the financial management. Examples are given here to help you in preparing an organization chart for your business.

In the beginning, the president of the small manufacturing company probably does everything.

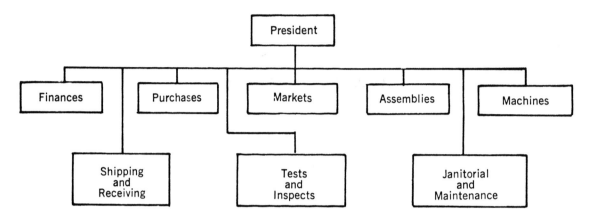

As the company grows to perhaps 50—100 employees, the organization may begin to look something like the chart below.

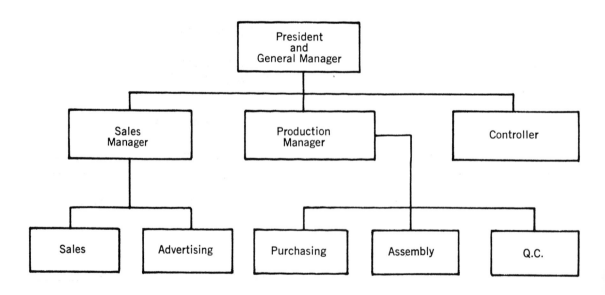

In the space that follows or on a separate piece of paper, draw an organization chart for your business.

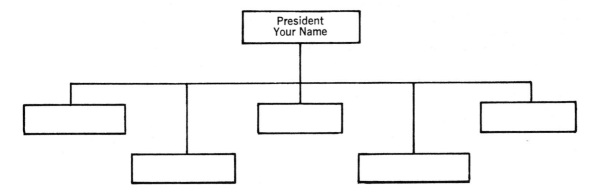

It is important that you recognize your weaknesses early in the game and plan to get assistance wherever you need it. This may be done by using consultants on an as-needed basis, by hiring the needed personnel, or by retaining a lawyer and accountant.

The workblock below lists some of the areas you may want to consider. Adapt it to your needs and indicate who will take care of the various functions. (One name may appear more than once.)

Manufacturing   _____

Marketing   _____

Research and Technical Backup   _____

Accounting   _____

Legal   _____

Insurance   _____

Other:

_____   _____

_____   _____

_____   _____

MAKING YOUR PLAN WORK

To make your plan work you will need feedback. For example, the year end profit and loss statement shows whether your business made a profit or loss for the past 12 months.

But you can't wait 12 months for the score. To keep your plan on target you need readings at frequent intervals. A profit and loss statement at the end of each month or at the end of each quarter is one type of frequent feedback. However, the P and L may be more of a *loss* than a profit statement if you rely only on it. In addition, your cash flow projection must be continuously updated and revised as necessary. You must set up management controls which will help you to insure that the right things are being done from day to day and from week to week.

The management control system which you set up should give you precise information on: inventory, production, quality, sales, collection of accounts receivable, and disbursements. The simpler the system, the better. Its purpose is to give you and your key people current information in time to correct deviations from approved policies, procedures, or practices. You are after *facts* with emphasis on *trouble spots*.

INVENTORY CONTROL. The purpose of controlling inventory is to provide maximum service to your customers. Your aim should be to achieve a rapid turnover on your inventory. The fewer dollars you tie up in raw materials inventory and in finished goods inventory, the better. Or, saying it in reverse, the faster you get back your investment in raw materials and finished goods inventory, the faster you can reinveset your capital to meet additional consumer needs.

In setting up inventory controls, keep in mind that the cost of the inventory is not your only cost. There are inventory costs, such as the cost of purchasing, the cost of keeping inventory records, and the cost of receiving and storing raw materials.

PRODUCTION. In preparing this business plan, you have estimated the cost figures for your manufacturing operation. Use these figures as the basis for standards against which you can measure your day-to-day operations to make sure that the clock does not nibble away at profits. These standards will help you to keep machine time, labor man-hours, process time, delay time, and down time within your projected cost figures. Periodic production reports will allow you to keep your finger on potential drains on your profits and should also provide feedback on your overhead expense.

QUALITY CONTROL. Poorly made products cause a company to lose customers. In addition, when a product fails to perform satisfactorily, shipments are held up, inventory is increased, and a severe financial strain can result. Moreover, when quality is poor, it's a good bet that waste and spoilage on the production line are greater than they should be. The details—checkpoints, reports, and so on—of your quality control system will depend on your type of production system. In working out these details, keep in mind that their purpose is to answer one question: What needs to be done to see that the work is done right the first time? Will you have to do extensive quality control on raw materials? This is an added expense you must consider.

SALES. To keep on top of sales, you will need answers to questions, such as:
How many sales were made? What was the dollar amount? What products were sold? At what price? What delivery dates were promised? What credit terms were given to customers?

It is also important that you set up an effective collection system for "accounts receivable," so that you don't tie up your capital in aging accounts.

DISBURSEMENTS. Your management controls should also give you information about the dollars your company pays out. In checking on your bills, you do not want to be penny-wise and pound-foolish. You need to know that major items, such as paying bills on time to get the supplier's discount, are being handled according to your policies. Your review system should also give you the opportunity to make judgments on the use of funds. In this manner, you can be on top of emergencies as well as routine situations. Your system should also keep you aware that tax moneys, such as payroll income tax deductions, are set aside and paid out at the proper time.

BREAK EVEN. Break-even analysis is a management control device because the break-even point shows about how much you must sell under given conditions in order to just cover your costs with NO profit and NO loss.

In preparing to start or expand a manufacturing business you should determine at what approximate level of sales a new product will pay for itself and begin to bring in a profit.

Profit depends on sales volume, selling price, and costs. So, to figure your break-even point, first separate your fixed costs, such as rent or depreciation allowance, from your variable costs per unit, such as direct labor and materials.

The formula is

$$\text{break-even volume} = \frac{\text{total fixed costs}}{\text{selling price} - \text{variable cost per unit}}$$

For example, Ajax Plastics has determined its fixed costs to be \$100,000 and variable costs to be \$50 per unit. If the selling price per unit is \$100, then Ajax's break-even volume is

$$\text{break-even volume} = \frac{\$100,000}{\$100 - \$50} = 2000 \text{ units}$$

On page 9 of this *Aid* you estimated your expected sales for each product and total sales. In the space below, compute the break-even point for each.

Product 1: _____ Product 2: _____ Total Sales: _____

For additional information on break-even points, see SBMS No. 15,
A Handbook of Small Business Finance in "For Further Information."

KEEPING YOUR PLAN UP TO DATE

The best made business plan gets out of date because conditions change. Sometimes the change is within your company, for example, several of your skilled operators quit their jobs. Sometimes the change is with customers. Their desires and tastes shift. For example, a new idea can sweep the country in 6 months and die overnight. Sometimes the change is technological as when new raw materials and components are put on the market.

In order to adjust a business plan to account for such changes, an owner-manager must:

(1) Be alert to the changes that come about in his company, in his industry, in his market, and in his community.

(2) Check his plan against these changes.

(3) Determine what revisions, if any, are needed in his plan.

You may be able to delegate parts of this work. For example, you might assign your shop foreman the task of watching for technical changes as reported in trade journals for your industry. Or you might expect your sales manager to keep you abreast of significant changes that occur in your markets.

But you cannot delegate the hardest part of this work. You cannot delegate the decisions as to what revisions will be made in your plan. As owner-manager you have to make those judgments on an on-going basis.

When judgments are wrong, cut your losses as soon as possible and learn from the experience. The mental anguish caused by wrong judgments is part of the price you pay for being your own boss. You get your rewards from the satisfaction and profits that result from correct judgments.

Sometimes, serious problems can be anticipated and a course of action planned. For example, what if sales are 25 percent lower than you anticipated, or costs are 10 percent higher? You have prepared what you consider a reasonable budget. It might be a good idea to prepare a "problem budget," based on either lower sales, higher costs, or a combination of the two.

You will also have to exercise caution if your sales are higher than you anticipated. The growth in sales may only be temporary. Plan your expansion. New equipment and additional personnel could prove to be crippling if sales return to their normal level.

Keep in mind that few owner-managers are right 100 percent of the time. They can improve their batting average by operating with a business plan and by keeping that plan up to date.

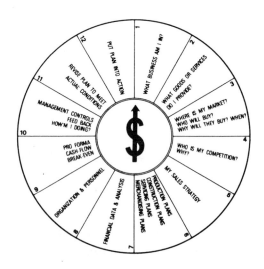

FOR FURTHER INFORMATION

The following references provide additional information about the various aspects of a business plan. This list is necessarily brief and selective. However, no slight is intended towards authors whose works are not mentioned.

Financial Statements of Small Business. S. B. Costales, 18 Ventura Drive, Danielson, Conn. 06239.

Annual Statement Studies. The Robert Morris Associates, Philadelphia National Bank Building, Philadelphia, Pa. 19107.

Key Business Ratios. Dun & Bradstreet, Inc., 99 Church St., New York, N. Y. 10008 (usually available in local Dun & Bradstreet offices).

Up Your Own Organization. Dible, Donald. 1971. The Entrepreneur Press, Mission Station, Drawer 2759, Santa Clara, Calif. 95051.

Thomas' Register of American Manufacturers. Annual (8 vols. and index). Thomas Publishing Company, 461 Eighth Ave., New York, N. Y. 10001.

OCCUPATIONAL SAFETY AND HEALTH ADMINISTRATION

Standards for General Industry. For sale by Superintendent of Documents, U.S. Government Printing Office, Washington, D.C. 20402, or a field office of the Occupational Safety and Health Administration.

BUREAU OF THE CENSUS

The Bureau of the Census issues a catalog listing of their many publications. The catalog is issued quarterly, with monthly supplements, available from the Superintendent of Documents, Washington, D. C. 20402. Ask for *Bureau of Census Catalog.* Annual subscription.

SMALL BUSINESS ADMINISTRATION

The following booklets are published by the Small Business Administration. They can be examined in the nearest SBA office or ordered from the Superintendent of Documents, Washington, D. C. 20402.

A Handbook of Small Business Finance. SBMS No. 15, 8th ed. 1965.
Ratio Analysis for Small Business. SBMS No. 20, 3d ed. 1970.
Management Audit for Small Manufacturers. SBMS No. 29.

The following *Management Aids* and *Small Business Bibliographies* are published by the Small Business Administration and are available free from the nearest SBA office:

"Numerical Control for the Smaller Manufacturer." MA No. 181.
"Using Census Data in Small Plant Marketing." MA 187.
"Should You Make Or Buy Components?" MA No. 189.
"What Is The Best Selling Price?" MA No. 193.
"Profile Your Customers To Expand Industrial Sales." MA 192.
"Marketing Planning Guidelines." MA No. 194.
"Are Your Products And Channels Producing Sales?" MA No. 203.
"Keep Pointed Toward Profit." MA No. 206.
"Pointers On Scheduling Production." MA No. 207.
"The Equipment Replacement Decision." MA No. 212.
"Marketing Research Procedures," SBB 9.
"National Directories for Use in Marketing," SBB 13.

Appendix Two
Going Public?

Should Your Company Go Public?

Healthy, growing companies frequently need additional funds to reach immediate goals. Going public is a popular, usually effective but sometimes burdensome way to obtain them.

It is not a decision to be reached lightly. It can be ideal for your company but it can also be costly, even critical, to your company's future.

Before taking such a step, seek expert advice. Talk to your attorney, your commercial and investment bankers and your CPAs. Because your accountants know a great deal about your company, they can be particularly helpful to you in reaching your decision on offering stock to the public.

Here are some possible advantages and disadvantages of going public, not only to your company but to its stockholders. Read them carefully and discuss them with your advisors before making a move.

POSSIBLE BENEFITS TO THE COMPANY

- Additional working capital is provided.
- Funds can be obtained for acquisitions, for retirement of short-term or long-term debts, for retirement of outstanding senior capital stock, for research and development, for expansion and diversification, for new equipment, and for plant modernization.
- Sale of stock or bonds on the public market establishes an effective method of valuing these securities.
- Stocks or bonds of a publicly-held company can be used for acquisitions and mergers while securities of a privately-held company are usually unacceptable.
- Sale of stock improves the debt to equity ratio, enhancing the ability to borrow.
- Favorable performance of your stock will improve your ability to sell future public issues of stock or bonds on favorable terms.
- Stock options may be used to recruit or retain exceptionally well-qualified executives.
- A public market for your company's stock can enhance your corporate image, and improve your public relations.

From a booklet presented by the Special Committee to Study Displacement of CPA Firms of the American Institute of Certified Public Accountants. Reproduced courtesy of the American Institute of Certified Public Accountants.

■ Ownership of stock in your company can generate more interest in it by customers, suppliers, employees and business associates.

POSSIBLE BENEFITS TO STOCKHOLDERS

■ With a public market, present stockholders will find it easier to dispose of a portion of their interest in the company to diversify their investment portfolio or for other reasons.

■ A public offering of stock in a previously closely-held company usually enhances its value.

■ A public market provides a basis for valuation of the company's stock. This valuation is necessary in establishing individual net worth and in connection with gift and inheritance taxes.

■ Executors of a stockholder's estate are able to liquidate the company's stock more readily to pay taxes, other debts, and bequests.

■ A public market usually offers protection to minority stockholders. It enables them to sell the company's stock more easily.

■ In many cases, stock in a publicly-held company provides a more secure investment for retirement.

POSSIBLE DISADVANTAGES TO THE COMPANY

■ Financial and other information not ordinarily disclosed by privately-held companies will now be available to competitors, customers, employees and others.

■ Paper work will increase because SEC regulations require detailed reporting. Formal board and stockholder meetings must be held and periodic financial reports issued.

■ Pressure from stockholders to maintain or steadily increase earnings and dividends may lead to short-term decisions that are harmful to the long-term welfare of the company.

■ Selling securities to the public can be expensive.

POSSIBLE DISADVANTAGES TO STOCKHOLDERS

■ Present stockholders may lose control of the company.

■ Major stockholders, officers and directors become subject to detailed SEC reporting requirements.

■ The freedom of the present stockholders to deal with the firm may be severely curtailed—for example, with respect to borrowing from the company by insiders.

■ The company's management can be sued by dissident stockholders who may claim insider transactions or conflicts of interest.

■ The freedom to utilize partnerships, multiple corporate arrangements or family trusts to reduce income taxes is lost.

Alternative sources of capital, not involving the public sale and public ownership of your company's securities, may also be available. Before you arrive at a final decision regarding a public offering, ask your CPA firm to assist you by exploring with your commercial and investment bankers how best to finance your needs.

Among the many sources of funds are:

■ Short-term and long-term unsecured loans from banks, insurance companies, or other private lenders.

■ Loans secured by real estate mortgages, chattel mortgages on equipment, or warehouse receipts.

■ Factoring or sale of accounts receivable.

■ Loans against the cash value of life insurance.

■ Loans from the Small Business Administration or from Small Business Investment Companies.

■ Sale and lease-back arrangements involving plant and equipment.

■ Private sale of securities under conditions exempt from regulation by the SEC.

Each of these methods has its advantages and its drawbacks. Your CPA firm can help you analyze each possibility in relation to your company's specific requirements.

Timing of a Public Offering

The timing of a public offering is of crucial importance and you will do well to heed the advice of your underwriters on the subject. Success of an offering requires that the company, the market and the investing public be ready.

Investigating the answers to the following questions may help you to determine the state of readiness of your company and the investment market.

■ Has the company shown long and consistent record of sales and earnings?

■ Do sales and earnings show a healthy growth pattern?

- Are the prospects for growth of sales and earnings good?

- Do earnings and sales growth compare favorably with other companies in the industry?

- Will investors be satisfied that the company has effective management?

- Is the state of the economy favorable?

- Is the stock market strong and rising?

- Are new issues currently being fully subscribed?

Of course, if your offering is especially attractive, your underwriter may suggest that you proceed even though stock market conditions are not entirely favorable.

In any case, following the underwriters advice on the timing of your offering is essential to success.

Advance Preparation For a Public Offering

If you are thinking about making a public offering within the next few years, now is the time to start assembling the team to help you—underwriters, CPAs and attorneys. They can give you professional guidance on the essential preliminary steps to registration.

The SEC requires that each registration statement and prospectus include a five year summary of earnings if your company has been in business that long. The Commission requires that the last three years be audited but many underwriters prefer to have all five years audited.

At this time, therefore, you may wish to consider making certain accounting changes that are acceptable to the SEC in first offerings because they make your company's financial statements more comparable to those of other publicly-held companies.

Your CPA firm can help you identify desirable changes in items such as reporting results of discontinued activities and others.

PRELIMINARY SUMMARY OF EARNINGS

When you approach underwriters regarding a prospective public offering by your company it is helpful if there is an impressive record of consistent earnings growth. However, a dip in earnings during the last five years need not be fatal. Your CPA firm can assist you in the preparation of such a preliminary five-year earnings summary and in its presentation to the underwriters.

OTHER IMPORTANT CONSIDERATIONS

The actual application for registration of your offering will be prepared by your legal counsel who, working with your CPA firm and staff, will see that all SEC requirements concerning corporate records, both legal and financial, are properly presented. This team, together with the underwriters, can also help you to determine the proper form of capitalization for your company and its conformance with SEC regulations.

Selecting and Working With the Managing Underwriter

The selection of the right managing underwriter is a critical decision. It can mean the difference between success or failure of your offering. A properly selected underwriter can ensure adequate distribution of your public offering and will endeavor to maintain a strong market for your company's securities after they are in public hands.

The qualities that should be considered in choosing the managing underwriter are:

■ Does the underwriting firm have a reputation for integrity and high standards of performance?

■ How effective has it been in other first public offerings?

■ Will it take a strong interest in your firm?

A good choice of underwriter can be the beginning of a mutually advantageous and enduring relationship. A poor choice can be laden with serious consequences.

Frequently, an initial offering is followed by other public offerings by the company or original stockholders. A managing underwriter who has become familiar with your company's operations and management by handling one public offering, often can expedite subsequent issues.

Your commercial bank, your attorneys, and your CPA firm can supply information about underwriting firms. Your CPA firm can even make preliminary inquiries to ascertain which underwriters may be interested in handling your public offering.

It is not wise to "shop around" too much when selecting an underwriter because many underwriting firms will lose interest even though the underwriting field is quite competitive. Consequently, some companies negotiate with only one underwriter. However, others find it beneficial to approach a second underwriting firm to obtain another point of view regarding alternate financing methods, marketability of the company's stock, offering-price ranges, and the form and amount of underwriter compensation.

The underwriting firm you select may be national, regional, or local, partly depending on the nature, scope, and contemplated distribution of your offering. If nationwide distribution of your public offering is not contemplated, you may wish to consider local or regional underwriters. They may be more familiar with your company and more interested in its operations. Even if national distribution is desired, many local and regional underwriters can arrange a nationwide underwriting syndicate.

COMPENSATING THE UNDERWRITER

The underwriter is compensated for his efforts in a number of ways, the basic one being a discount or commission. The underwriter undertakes to sell your company's stock at an agreed price and he obtains the stock from your company at a discount. The difference between the price paid by the underwriter and the offering price to the public represents the underwriter's commission.

Sometimes, an underwriter will ask for warrants or options to buy additional shares of stock at a specified price. The underwriter may also ask for "bargain" stock or a specified amount for expenses of the underwriting. However, many underwriters confine their compensation to the underwriter's discount or commission. believing that unfavorable connotations may flow from other forms of compensation.

Your CPA firm can compile comparative data on underwriter's commissions and other income from recent public offer-ings that will assist you in evaluating the total compensation requested by the underwriter.

The underwriter may make a "fixed commitment" to purchase a specific number of shares of the proposed offering at an agreed price. On the other hand, the underwriter may make no firm commitment and merely undertake to exercise his "best efforts" to sell your company's shares. or to market the offering on an "all or none" basis. Obviously, without a firm commitment, you have no assurance that adequate financing. or any financing at all, will result.

All terms of the agreement with the underwriter are open for negotiation. If your company is well-established, financially sound. and has a consistent earning record; if the public is interested in the kind of business conducted by your company. and if stock market conditions are strong. you are in a better position to hold out for favorable terms. On the other hand, if your company is untried and its stock is rated as highly speculative, your bargaining position is weakened.

In any event, it is prudent to have your attorneys and your CPA firm present during discussions with the underwriter. They can be invaluable in working out equitable terms and avoiding unfavorable commitments such as too low a price range, too high an underwriter's commission, undue restrictions or concessions, or undesirable forms of underwriter compensation.

Pricing Your First Public Offering

The proposed price range and the final price of your public offering is the result of negotiation between the managing underwriter and the company. The underwriter has had a great deal of experience in pricing first issues and his opinion should be given considerable weight.

Obviously, a high price appeals to the selling company. However, overpricing should be avoided as it can have both immediate and long-term bad effects. If overpriced, the issue may be difficult to sell. After issue, the market price may decline and it may take a long time to revive the interest of the investing public in your company's stock. The ideal situation is a public offering so priced that the stock will show a modest increase in price after distribution has been completed.

Occasionally, the price realized on the sale of the public offering is higher than the price initially proposed by the underwriter.

Since it is impractical to agree on a firm price until just before the security is publicly offered, preliminary proposals by the underwriter usually take the form of a price range. Immediately after the registration is declared effective by the SEC, the final offering price is negotiated by the underwriter and the company and the stock is offered for sale to the public.

The most significant factor in arriving at the price of your first public offering is the earnings per share of your company as compared with similar companies publicly held. Other important factors are the growth rate of your company's sales and earnings, the prevailing stock market conditions, and the interest of the investing public in new issues.

A realistic proposed price range is best arrived at by the use of a comparative pricing schedule. Your CPA firm can prepare this for you. It compares your company with similar companies already on the market in such vital areas as:

■ Market on which traded.

■ Number of shares of common which will be outstanding if all securities convertible into common shares are converted.

■ Capitalization: long-term debt, minority interests, preferred stock, and common stock.

■ Current ratio and debt-to-equity ratio.

■ Gross revenues for the five most recent years, estimated revenues for the year in progress and the rate of gross revenue growth for the same period.

■ Net income and earnings per share (before and after dilution by convertible securities) for the five-year period, and rates of growth.

■ Ratios of net income for the most recent full year to gross revenues, total assets, equity of common stock, and total capitalization including long-term debt.

- Most recent market price of common stock, equity per share of common stock, and ratio of market price to equity.

- Price to earnings ratio on common stock (before and after dilution by convertible securities) for the most recent fiscal year and estimated for the year in progress.

- Dividend yield on common stock for the most recent fiscal year and estimated for the year in progress.

Other factors which affect the price of your first public offering are:

- Dilution of future earnings per share which will result from the sale of the new shares.

- Effect on future earnings of the proposed uses of the new funds.

- Investors' assessment of management, standing of the company, labor supply, labor relations (strike proneness), plant and equipment in comparison with competition, vulnerability to competition, acquisition and expansion policies, and size of the public issue.

Cost of Going Public

The main cost of a public offering is the underwriter's total compensation. One element of this compensation, the underwriter's discount or commission, has ranged around 7% to 10% on recent stock offerings of from one to five million dollars. On some larger issues of over ten million dollars it has been as low as 5% on stock offerings and 1¼% on debentures. In addition, there may be special forms of underwriter compensation such as "bargain" stock, options, warrants, or a contribution to the expenses of sale. These special forms of compensation must be evaluated to ascertain the underwriter's total compensation.

The underwriter's discount and special forms of compensation will vary depending on whether the issue is common stock or debentures, its size, and his assessment of the difficulty of selling your public offering.

In addition to the underwriter's compensation, other expenses will range from about 1½% to 5% on a public stock offering of between one and five million dollars. These other expenses include:

- Cost of printing the registration statement, prospectus, underwriting agreement, and other documents.

- SEC and Blue Sky registration or filing fees.

- Stock or bond certificates.

- Registrar and transfer agent fees.

- Federal issue tax.

- Insurance to protect underwriters and selling stockholders against suits under the Federal Securities Act. (This insurance is not always available.)

- Legal and accounting fees.

Legal and accounting fees will depend on the complexity of the company's operation. If this is your first public offering they will be substantial, particularly if your company's financial statements have not been audited for at least the last three years.

Role of Your Accounting Firm

Your CPA knows your company, your industry, and the financial data which must be presented effectively to carry your offering through to a successful sale. He can provide you with valuable assistance throughout the entire process of going public by:

- Evaluating the benefits and disadvantages of going public.

- Helping you with your planning and your initial preparation (see section on Advance Preparation For a Public Offering).

- Approaching underwriters to ascertain their interest in your public offering.

- Compiling data to evaluate the compensation proposed by the underwriter.

- Providing consultation and advice in your negotiations with the underwriter concerning financial matters to be included in a letter of intent and in the final underwriting agreement.

- Arranging for a pre-filing conference with the SEC if considered necessary.

- Helping you prepare the required financial data and auditing your financial statements.

- Participating with you, your attorney and the underwriter in the preparation of the registration statement and the prospectus.

- Reviewing proofs of the registration statement and prospectus.

- Revising the financial information in the registration statement and prospectus if required by the SEC.

- Furnishing a "comfort letter" to assure the underwriters that there were no material adverse changes in the financial information included in the registration statement after it was filed with the SEC.

If your present outside auditors are independent, adequately staffed, and capable of complying with the requirements of the SEC, they should handle the presentation of your financial statements and other supporting schedules in the registration statement filed with the Commission. Their knowledge of your operations can be very valuable in speeding the preparation of the registration statement and in helping you "put your best foot forward" in connection with your public offering.

Underwriters sometimes request that

your present outside auditors be displaced by a nationally-known accounting firm. However, a great many underwriters will not propose displacement of the company's present accounting firm if it is independent, adequately staffed, and capable of complying with SEC requirements. These underwriters are satisfied that neither the formation of the underwriting syndicate nor the offering price is affected by the choice of auditors.

The SEC encourages all firms meeting its requirements to engage in registration work and has indicated concern over the unjustified displacement of accounting firms at the suggestion of some underwriters. Over 500 accounting firms, other than nationals, served as the principal accountants on registration statements filed and becoming effective in a recent year. More are being added each year to the list of firms that are qualified by experience to do SEC work and many underwriters are beginning to recognize this fact.

AN UNDERWRITER'S VIEW

One underwriting firm of national reputation sends each new first-offering client a statement about the selection of independent CPAs which has this to say about going public and the expertise.

manpower and independence required of accountants in this work:

In the course of bringing forth public offerings we are often asked if there are special requirements in selecting independent certified public accountants for this purpose. Our answer in brief is this.

"Going public introduces new accounting responsibilties to the conduct of business. Annual and periodic reports will have to be filed with the SEC in forms prescribed by that Commission and in accordance with their rules and regulations. Further, in presenting a proposed offering to the SEC, sound guidance by independent certified public accountants experienced in such work is most important. Competence in SEC matters, then, is a primary requisite. Underwriters and investment bankers have found that national accounting firms and many local or regional accounting firms have this competence. It is not necessary that the firm be national, but it is necessary that it be competent in SEC work.

"A public offering can also be very demanding of accounting manpower. An offering may involve many accounting complexities and usually requires the assemblage of a great amount of accounting data within short periods of time to meet tight schedules for submission of reports. The accounting firm, therefore, should have sufficient manpower to meet these needs. Your present CPA firm, whether national or local, may have the necessary manpower as well as the competence described earlier. Further, you should consider the familiarity your present firm has with your business, its history and background. This can be a very valuable additional factor in speeding the progress of the work and facilitating the functions of the underwriter.

"Whether the accounting firm selected is national, regional or local, the underwriter will charge the same discount or commission for his services and will price the stock in the same way—in accordance with the market value of the business.

"P.S. It goes without saying that the accounting firm must meet the SEC requirements of 'independence."

YOUR GOING PUBLIC TEAM

In view of this statement, now is the time for you to discuss going public with both your CPAs and your attorneys. Find out whether they have the competence, manpower, independence and financial responsibility to take you through a public offering or whether they can retain the assistance necessary from firms that are qualified. If they have the needed characteristics or can acquire them, with the assistance of other firms, then plan to keep them as members of your going public team.

If when going public a company going public makes a strong stand for retention of its present CPA firm for the registration, the underwriter will in most instances go along with the choice.

Glossary

Accelerated depreciation. A method of depreciation that charges off more of the original cost of the fixed assets in the earlier years than in the later years of the asset's service life.

Account. A recording unit used to reflect the changes in assets, liabilities, or owners' equity.

Account receivable. An amount that is owed to the business, usually by one of its customers, as a result of the ordinary extension of credit.

Accounting period. The period of time over which an income statement summarizes the changes in owners' equity; usually, the period is one year.

Accrual basis. The measurement of revenues and expenses, as contrasted with receipts and expenditures.

Accrued expense. A liability arising because an expense occurs in a period prior to the related expenditure.

Accumulated depreciation. An account showing the total amount of depreciation of an asset that has been accumulated to date.

Acid-test ratio. The ratio obtained by dividing quick assets by current liabilities.

Allowance for doubtful accounts. The amount of estimated bad debts that is subtracted from accounts receivable on the balance sheet.

Amortization. The process of writing off the cost of intangible assets; similar to depreciation.

Asset. An item which is owned by the business and has a value that can be measured objectively.

Auditing. A review of accounting records by independent, outside public accountants.

Bad debts. The estimated amount of credit sales that will not be collected.

Balance. The difference between the totals of the two sides of an account.

Balance sheet. A financial statement which reports the assets and equities of a company at one point in time. Assets are listed on the left and equities on the right.

Bond. A written promise to repay money furnished to the business, with interest, at some future date, usually five or more years hence.

Capital stock. A balance sheet account showing the amount that was assigned to the shares of stock at the time they were originally issued.

Capital turnover. A ratio obtained by dividing annual sales by investment.

Cash basis accounting. An accounting system that does not use the accrual basis.

Closing. The transfer of the balance from one account to another account.

Common stock. Stock whose owners are not entitled to preferential treatment with regard to dividends or to the distribution of assets in the event of liquidation; usually, common stockholders control the company.

Cost accounting. The process of identifying manufacturing costs and assigning them to inventory in the manufacturing process.

Cost concept. Assets are ordinarily valued at the price paid to acquire them.

Cost of goods sold. The cost of the merchandise sold to customers.

Credit. The right-hand side of an account, or an amount entered on the right-hand side of an account.

Creditor. A person who lends money or extends credit to a business.

Current assets. Assets which are either currently in the form of cash or are expected to be converted into cash within a short period of time (usually one year).

Current liabilities. Obligations which become due within a short period of time (usually one year).

Current ratio. The ratio obtained by dividing the total of the current assets by the total of the current liabilities.

Days' receivables. The number of days of sales that are tied up in accounts receivable.

Debt. The left-hand side of an account, or an amount entered on the left-hand side of an account.

Debt capital. The capital raised by the issuance of bonds.

Debt ratio. The ratio obtained by dividing debt capital by total capital.

Deferred revenue. The liability that arises when a customer pays a business in advance for a service or product. It is a liability because the business has an obligation to render the service or deliver the product.

Depletion. The process of writing off the cost of a wasting asset.

Depreciation. The process of recognizing a portion of the cost of an asset as an expense during each year of its estimated service life.

Direct labor or material. The labor or material that is used directly on a product.

Dividend. The funds generated by profitable operations that are distributed to the shareholders.

Double-declining balance method. An accelerated method of depreciation.

Double-entry system. A characteristic of accounting in which each transaction recorded causes at least two changes in the accounts.

Dual aspect concept. The accounting concept which assumes that the total assets of a company always equal the total equities.

Earnings. Another term for net income.

Earnings per share. A ratio obtained by dividing the total earnings for a given period by the number of shares of common stock outstanding.

Entity concept. The accounting concept which assumes that accounts are kept for business entities, rather than for the persons who own, operate, or are otherwise associated with the business.

Entry. The accounting record made for a single transaction.

Equities. Claims against assets that are held by owners or by creditors.

Equity capital. The capital raised from owners.

Expenditure. An amount arising from the acquisition of an asset.

Expense. A decrease in owners' equity resulting from operations.

FIFO. The first-in, first-out inventory method which assumes that the goods that enter the inventory first are the first to be sold.

Fixed assets. The tangible properties of relatively long life that are generally used in the production of goods and services, rather than being held for resale.

Going-concern concept. The accounting concept which assumes that a business will continue to operate indefinitely.

Goodwill. An intangible asset; an amount paid for a favorable location or reputation.

Gross margin. The difference between sales revenue and cost of goods sold.

Income statement. A statement of revenues and expenses for a given period.

Interim statements. Financial statements prepared for a period of less than one year.

Inventories. Goods being held for sale, and material and partially finished products which will be sold upon completion.

Inventory turnover. Tells how many times inventory was totally replaced during the year; calculated by dividing the average inventory into cost of goods sold.

Investments. Securities that are held for a relatively long period of time and are purchased for reasons other than the temporary use of excess cash. They are noncurrent assets.

Journal. A record in which entries are recorded in chronological order.

Lease. An agreement under which the owner of property permits someone else to use it.

Ledger. A group of accounts.

Liability. The equity or claim of a creditor.

LIFO. The last-in, first-out inventory method which assumes that the last goods purchased are the first to be sold.

Liquid assets. Cash and assets which are easily converted into cash.

Liquidity ratios. The relationship of obligations soon coming due to assets which should provide the cash for meeting these obligations.

Manufacturing overhead. All manufacturing costs that are not direct material or direct labor.

Market value. The amount for which an asset can be sold in the marketplace.

Marketable securities. Securities that are expected to be converted into cash within a year; a current asset.

Matching concept. Costs are matched against the revenue of a period.

Materiality concept. Disregard trivial matters; disclose all important matters.

Money measurement concept. A concept that assumes that accounting records show only facts that can be expressed in monetary terms.

Mortgage. A pledge of real estate as security for a loan.

Net book value. The difference between the cost of a fixed asset and its accumulated depreciation.

Net income. The amount by which total revenues exceed total expenses for a given period.

Net loss. The amount by which total expenses exceed total revenues for a given period.

Nominal account. An income statement account that is closed at the end of the period to a balance sheet account.

Noncurrent liability. A claim which does not fall due within one year.

Note receivable. An amount owed that is evidenced by a promissory note.

Obsolescence. A loss in the usefulness of an asset because of the development of improved equipment, changes in style, or other causes not related to the physical condition of the asset.

Operating expenses. Costs associated with sales and administrative activities as distinct from those associated with production of goods or services.

Overhead rate. A rate used to allocate overhead costs to products.

Owners' equity. The claims of owners against the assets of a business.

Paid in capital. An amount in excess of the par or stated value of stock that is paid by investors.

Par value. The specific amount printed on the face of a stock certificate.

Partnership. An unincorporated business with two or more owners.

Period costs. Costs associated with general sales and administrative activities.

Permanent capital. Debt and equity capital.

Perpetual inventory. An individual record of the cost of each item in inventory.

Physical inventory. The counting of all merchandise currently on hand.

Posting. The process of transferring transactions from the journal to the ledger.

Preferred stock. Stock whose owners receive preferential treatment with regard to dividends or with regard to the distribution of assets in the event of liquidation.

Prepaid expenses. Services and certain intangibles purchased prior to the period during which their benefits are received; treated as assets until they are consumed.

Price-earnings ratio. A ratio obtained by dividing the average market price of the stock by the earnings per share.

Product costs. Costs associated with the manufacture of products.

Profit. See net income.

Profit margin. Net income expressed as a percentage of net sales.

Proprietorship. An unincorporated business with a single owner.

Quick assets. Current assets other than inventory and prepaid expenses.

Real account. An account with a balance after the closing process has been completed; it appears on the balance sheet.

Realization concept. An accounting concept which assumes that revenue is recognized when goods are delivered or services are performed, in an amount that is reasonably certain to be realized.

Recognize. The act of recording a revenue or expense item in a given accounting period.

Residual value. The amount for which a company expects to be able to sell a fixed asset at the end of its service life.

Retained earnings. The increase in the shareholders' equity as a result of profitable company operations.

Return. The amount earned on invested funds during a period.

Return on shareholders' investment. A ratio obtained by dividing the return by the average amount of shareholders' investment for the period.

Revenue. An increase in owners' equity resulting from operations.

Security. An instrument such as a stock or bond.

Service life. The period of time over which an asset is estimated to be of service to the company.

Shareholders. The owners of an incorporated business.

Solvency. The ability to meet long-term obligations.

Stated value. The amount that the directors decide is the value of no-par stock.

Statement of changes in financial position. A financial statement explaining the changes that have occurred in asset, liability, and owners' equity items in an accounting period.

Stock split. An exchange of the number of shares of stock outstanding for a larger number.

Straight line method. A depreciation method which charges off an equal fraction of the cost of a fixed asset over each year of its service life.

Taxable income. The amount of income subject to income tax, computed according to the rules of the Internal Revenue Service.

Transaction. A business event that is recorded in the accounting records.

Treasury stock. Previously issued stock that has been bought back by the company.

Write down. To reduce the cost of an item, especially inventory, to its market value.

Years'-digit method. An accelerated method of depreciation.

Index